Gardens of Awe and Folly

A Traveler's Journal on the Meaning of Life and Gardening

Vivian Swift

Bloomsbury

New York   London   New Delhi   Oxford   Sydney

Bloomsbury USA
An imprint of Bloomsbury Publishing Plc

1385 Broadway   50 Bedford Square
New York   London
NY 10018   WC1B 3DP
USA   UK

www.bloomsbury.com

First published 2016

ISBN: HB: 978-1-63286-027-9
ebook   978-1-63286-028-6

LIBRARY OF CONGRESS CATALOGING-IN-PUBLICATION DATA HAS BEEN APPLIED FOR.

2 4 6 8 10 9 7 5 3 1

The entire text of this book has been typeset by hand by the author.

Printed and bound in China by C&C Offset Printing Co Ltd

To find out more about our authors and books visit www.bloomsbury.com. Here you will find
extracts, author interviews, details of forthcoming events and the option to sign up for our
newsletters.

Bloomsbury books may be purchased for business or promotional use. For information on bulk
purchases please contact Macmillan Corporate and Premium Sales Department at
specialmarkets@macmillan.com.

for

James Stone

my favorite gardener

Contents

If all you ask of a garden is *What?*,
then all you'll probably get in reply is a planting list.
But ask, instead,
Why? How? When? and, most of all, *Who?*,
and then you're in for a nice, long conversation.
This book is a collection of the conversations I've had
with nine gardens that had a lot to say.

Gardeners show us
what it is to live
in daily expectation of wonder.

Ancient Sufi proverb

Hidden in Plain Sight

Of course I had seen it many times before, that strange little forest floating just above the water's surface, right in the middle of the Seine.

But today I am taking myself across the Pont Neuf for a firsthand, person-to-garden experience with the Square du Vert-Galant, a weird urban woodland named in honor of France's most beloved king, Henri IV.

Good King Henri IV's nickname, the Vert Galant, isn't easily translatable even if you know that **vert** means "green" and **galant** means "gallant." **Green Gallant** is something that I will have to explain later.

In French **square** means "small public garden."

Behind the statue of Henri IV on the Pont Neuf there is a dark narrow staircase with 40 steep steps. This is how you descend 23 feet (7 meters) to get to the Square du Vert-Galant. The Square is the last remnant of the true, ancient ground level of Paris, the exact place where a tribe of Celts called the Parisii founded a fishing village two thousand years ago.

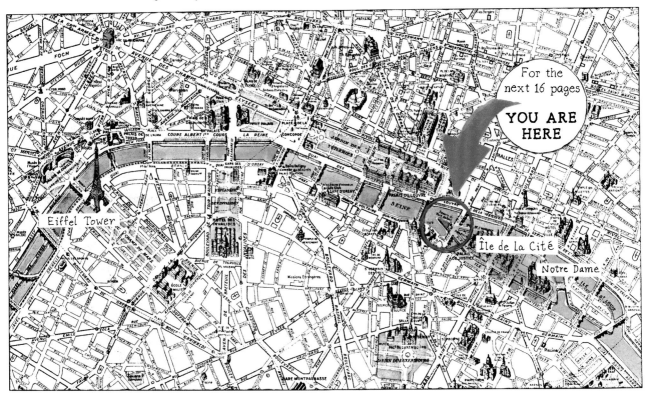

This historic bit of low-lying land has not been treated with any special reverence over the centuries. The Sun King Louis XIV toyed with the idea of building an enormous faux-Roman Forum here in 1662. Napoleon considered a proposal to erect a massive four-story spa on the site in 1804. Thereafter, it was turned over to small-time developers as a site of bathhouses and open-air theaters. It is fortunate indeed that sheer neglect preserved this space, intact, until 1885, when the City of Paris acquired it for a public garden.

Making a Grand Entrance
An Appreciation of the Garden Gate

If gardens are created to tell stories, which I believe they are, then garden gates are the crucial opening lines that can make or break a tale.

And as there are many styles of great opening lines, so are there many kinds of great garden gates:

Portentous   (*Call me Ishmael.*)
Awe-inspiring (*In the beginning God created the Heavens and the Earth.*)
Romantic (*Last night I dreamed I went to Manderley again...*)
Whimsical (*Here is Edward bear coming down the stairs...*)

The gate to the Square du Vert-Galant is instantly recognizable as **Poetic**, along the lines of *Ode on a Grecian Urn.*

You see, this a **Vase Gate**.

The shape is unmistakably that of a Chinese 10th-century Song Dynasty vase.

A traditional Chinese garden, being a meticulously composed series of landscapes, uses gates, shaped as full moons, willow leaves, fans, or vases, to give focus to the emotional and aesthetic intentions of the garden experience.

Now, I'm pretty sure that having a Chinese vase gate in this particular Paris garden is purely coincidental. But it gets the job done. It does feel necessary to pause here, to take in the view, and be made mindful of the landscape one is about to enter. If you should feel inclined to fall in love with this garden at first sight, now is the time and place.

The garden of the
Square du Vert-Galant
is tiny, only 2/3 of an acre
(2665 sq. meters).
But it feels **vast**.

The square feels much bigger than it really is because of its
island mentality. Surrounded by the waters of the River Seine,
isolated from its urban reality, the Square feels remote and
completely detached from the bedlam of current events.
It could even declare independence.
This garden would make a perfectly respectable **micro-nation**.

The towering trees that enclose the Square du Vert-Galant also throw off all sense of scale. The impression the trees give, of being a mighty old-growth forest, dwarfs the true proportions of this itty bitty garden.

And then there's the view. So much of France's history and patrimony is in sight: the Louvre, La Samaritaine, the Monnaie de Paris, the Institute de France; the distant dome of the Grand Palais, the Tour Eiffel. It's glorious and it's mind-boggling.

It all comes down to the Paris Effect.
Just being present in the limitless self-confidence that the city has in itself as the pinnacle of civilization has a way of making your own sense of self feel greatly enlarged, alert to the possibilities of transformation and greatness.

The Square du Vert-Galant is often described as being the prow of the ship that is the Île de la Cité. If so, the port side of the Square offers the more picturesque views of the river and the Left Bank. In sight is the Pont Neuf, the bridge that has made it possible to get on and off our little Parisii sandbar since 1606.

Some scholars say that the ancestor of the Eurasian Chestnut tree that looms over our view was brought to Gaul by the Romans, but the smart money is on a sapling transported from Constantinople in 1615 by a gentleman botanist named Bachelier. Although the Eurasian Chestnut conker is nearly identical to the edible *marron* of the European Sweet Chestnut, the two are totally unrelated -- one is from the lychee family of trees and the other is kin to the oak.

The great 19th-century urban planner of Paris, Georges-Eugène Haussmann, had a particular fondness for the Eurasian *Aesculus hippocastanum*. During his 17-year reign as the all-powerful Prefect of the Seine Haussmann had over 100,000 of them planted in city parks and along the *grands boulevards*.

In 1780, a gardener named M. Petigny paid the exorbitant price of 40 crowns ($800.00, € 620.00) for a (then) extremely rare *Gingko biloba* tree In remembrance of M. Petigny's folly, the Gingko biloba is still called the **40 Crown Tree** in France, and these days you can buy one for $49.95 (€ 39.00).

A *low, vulgar, disorderly* city -- Voltaire was disgusted by the Paris of his day: *stinking streets, ugly black houses, an air of filth, poverty, beggars* [etc.]. This riverbank was a sewage-covered swamp before the great Baron Haussmann eradicated the squalor of central Paris and transformed her into the City of Light. And now these riverbanks are highly desirable habitats.

Fourteen houseboats are permitted to berth here on the Quai de Conti. One of the boats serves as home base for the Paris Firemen River Brigade -- the on-duty *pompiers* dive into the Seine every morning at 9 AM for their daily swim around the Île de la Cité.

I've also heard tell that another one of these boats is home to a renowned philosopher/novelist who moved into his little *peniche* with four Persian cats, a wine cellar, and a Fazioli grand piano.

Some people just know how to live.

To some, it's just a fancy shed. To me, it's a Bijoux Chateau.

This *kiosque de garde* is the only structure in the entire garden. As soon as I saw it, it became my dream to inhabit it as my Paris *pied-a-terre*.

The kiosk is attributed to Gabriel Davioud, the chief architect of parks and gardens under Baron Haussmann. M. Davioud also designed the lampposts, benches, balustrades, fountains, and other street furnishings that comprise the human-scale elements of the city's magnificent Second Empire urban plan.

Prime Central Paris location, Beaux-Arts gem, Adorable Parisian Palace for One. The cozy 25 sq. ft.(2 3 sq. meter) octagonal open-floor plan is flooded with natural light. Exterior retains pristine period details (c. 1857); interior needs slight renovation.

My future Paris *chateau* was locked up tight when I stopped by to take measurements for curtains, but a peep through the front window revealed a dreary utilitarian space with dismal minimalist furnishings: a worn out schoolroom chair, a space heater, a 1970s two-way radio. The building's current occupants are the *gardiens* of the Square du Vert-Galant, making this the most charming office space in all of France. But *mon dieu!* This is not a *bureau* for civil servants! This is architecture worthy of the Lady of the *Locus Amoenus!* Moi.

The Square du Vert-Galant has all the makings of a micro-nation: It's got a stand-alone identity and a killer location. The Square deserves self-determination, with me as its Determiner-In-Residence, and I need a grande residence. This is the BEFORE picture. Turn the page for the AFTER.

The fringe benefit of reigning over the micro-nation of the
Square du Vert-Galant is having the garden all to yourself from
dawn until Opening Hour. Although the public has to be let in
at 8 AM, you've already had time enough to gather yourself in
the presence of Paris and take in the breadth of the day.

Go big.

Compose sixteen sonnets.

Invent dream cartography.

Save the polar bears.

The Tale of the Gallant Who Was Green

For most of the world, the color green is a very soothing background color, the hue of tranquility and emotional balance.

But in France, green has a lot more *oomph*. The French regard green as an especially lush and vivifying color.

Green is virile and robust. It's the color of romance and *l'amour*. It's why Henri IV was given the nickname **Vert Galant**, the *Green Gallant*.

The term **Vert Galant** is often translated as *rake, playboy, womanizer, whorehound, gay blade, lusty smooth-talker, old lecher*, etc.

All wrong.

Vert Galant means what it literally means, **green gentleman,** and yes, it's a mildly off-color term. But it is also completely acceptable for use by children -- something that *whorehound* is not.

During his reign (1589 - 1610) our good King Henri IV managed to break records for pitching woo. His scores of love affairs represent a heroic feat of amiability that the French admiringly view as *très très green*.

Considering that Henri IV was an elderly man in his mid-40s when he was crowned King of France, his middle-age prowess with the ladies was even *greener* than green.

It was **evergreen.**

And that is how this lovely patch of green in the heart of Paris came by its name, in honor of the *Vert Galant* and his ever-lasting gallantry in the very greenest things of life.

The Square du Vert-Galant is the most popular place in Paris to propose marriage.

Gardens
lend themselves to romance...

I'm even convinced that a garden's capacity
for inspiring romance should be a criterion
for evaluation in terms of horticultural excellence.

Alain Baraton, Gardener-in-Chief at the Palace of Versailles

Oh, yes indeed, the Square du Vert-Galant is a very romantic garden.
And anyone with a smidgen of imagination can see that the Weeping Willow
is its most romantic tree.

19

Of all the forests I have known
I wish to belong
where the willows are.

Ancient Celtic prayer
that I just made up.

There are stories that the ancient Celts used Weeping Willow twigs to bind magical and sacred objects together. Willow wands were waved by ancient poets to conjure up dreams, and prehistoric prophets wore Willow-woven crowns to enhance their visions. And I believe that none of these stories are true.

I'm pretty sure that all the "legendary" uses of the Weeping Willow are a lot of hooey, the product of wishful reverse-engineering by latter-day pagans.

But I understand the urge to mythologize the Weeping Willow. There's something about this tree that brings out the sentimental side of us humans. We can't help but experience the sway of willow branches as intentional, and alluring.

It is an extremely beautiful tree. The drapery of its foliage is the essence of grace, and is as delicate as a butterfly's mood swings. The change of color, as the fronds shimmer weightlessly in and out of the light, flickers from a blue-green moodiness to a joyful celadon sparkle.

I mean, *Wow*.

It's also a pleasantly melancholy tree. That sound you hear when a breeze rustles through the Weeping Willow's silky, lance-shaped leaves? I have it on good authority that it's Mozart's mournful *Lacrimosa* in D minor.

When We say *Adieu* to a Willow tree

A Weeping Willow that seems to be at its most stupendous state of being is, in fact, dying. Weeping Willows have only a short 50 to 70 year life span. As soon as they top out, it's time for them to go.

At the beginning of the 21st century the time had come for the magnificent old tree at the tip of the Square du Vert-Galant to go. If you were in Paris during those years, you no doubt saw the absurdly tiny replacement, and lucky you! What a sight!

There stood a pitiful twig, utterly dwarfed by the grandeur of its setting; a mere sprig engulfed by the absence of the colossus that had once stood there. And yet, for those of us who know how to project our own mind-expanding experience of Paris onto baby Willow trees, that sapling was already majestic, haloed by bright possibilities, radiant with the glow of its mission in life, afire with its destiny to uphold an historic place in the world.

Paris Gardening Tip:
Think Like a Micro-Nation

Every garden tells a story.
This is the story of the Square du Vert-Galant.

A garden here on the tip of the Île de la Cité was unthinkable back when there were 15,000 inhabitants crammed onto this teeny eyot. And then came one Georges-Eugène "Baron" Haussmann, a man who had the big -- *ridiculously* big -- idea of transforming miserable medieval Paris into a masterpiece of enlightened urban elegance. His overhaul began in 1853.

By the end of his career, in 1870, Haussmann had bulldozed every last slum in central Paris. He had cleared 333 miles of stinking alleyways, built 250 miles of sewers (lined with underground telephone cables), laid out 400 miles of paved avenues (whose sidewalks concealed underground electrical wires), and created 4,000 acres of parks and public gardens. He reduced the population on the Île de la Cité by 90%. The Île is currently home to 1,670 of the luckiest people in the world. *Vive la difference!*

The Paris that is so beloved today as the *nec plus ultra* of civilization is very much the Paris of Haussmann.

It is the force of Haussmann's colossal *idea* of Paris that suffuses every inch and moment In the Square du Vert-Galant with a sense of place that is as grand as it is feasible. That's the spirit I dream of taking to its logical conclusion, namely micro-nationhood, with me as its *grande dame*.

Big ideas in small places is what the garden of the Square du Vert-Galant is all about.

Here's what I think: If you ever start to feel as if yours is a measly 2/3 acre life, remember the Square du Vert-Galant.

And then nothing about you, your ideas, or your garden will ever feel small again.

Key West

Last Refuge
of a
Plant Kingdom Outlaw—

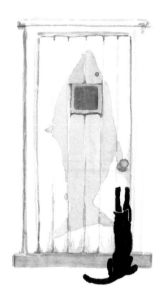

My Kind of Place

The forgiving tropical climate, isolation from the
mainland, a long history of looking the other way --
Key West is a foregone conclusion for anyone looking to
hide out or start over. A shady *joie de vivre* hangs in the
air like the scent of overripe sapodillas
(burnt sugar and old brandy wine).
It's an accepting and lenient way of life down here in
America's southernmost get-away-from-it-all.
Anything goes in Key West, except snivelling.

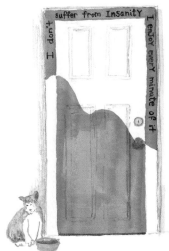

When Ernest Hemingway lived in Key West he was famous for three things: inventing the sugarless daiquiri, adoring the company of cats, and punching Wallace Stevens in the face. Thanks to Ernest's lasting influence it's a local custom that almost everything in Key West -- folding laundry, walking the dog, writing novels, voting -- goes hand-in-hand with an ice-cold rum cocktail, and there is an unwritten code that one must give absolute right of way to the town's many free range cats, on all public and private property.

And as for Wallace Stevens (an artsy modernist poet and a mean drunk), everyone said he had it coming.

Open invitation.

The time: Magic Hour.
The place: Old Town.
The Reason:
To be the still point of a
turning world.

Every evening
Key West throws a
sunset watching party
on
Mallory Square and
everyone --
tourists
non-tourists
fire-eaters
jugglers
psychics
seers
lonelyhearts
the weird and the reborn
the one-man bands
and
the visiting rum-soaked
merrymakers --
everyone
is welcome to
celebrate their
come-as-you-are
humanity
in an
ordinary and everyday
experience of awe.

The Green Parrot welcomes everyone with the same hearty bonhomie that it gives its regular
crowd of local renegades -- professors, vagabonds, novelists, millionaires, bikers, artists,
and all-night good-time guys and gals.
I order a Cuba Libre (served in a plastic cup, no umbrella) and am swapping life stories with
Charlie (AKA *Trigger Man*) when he pushes aside his house brand ale and woozily sketches a map
on the back of his coaster. *Fort Zach Park*, he explains. *Sunset. Go.*
I consider this a hot tip. Sunsets are serious business in Key West.

Fort Zachary Taylor Historic State Park is an 87-acre (35 hectare) National Historic
Landmark renowned for a moated fort built in 1845 as part of a manifest destiny defense strategy
for the southeastern U. S. coastline. The park is the only such landmark named for Major General
"Old Rough and Ready" Zachary Taylor, the hero of the Mexican-American War
and the 12th President of the United States. Taylor served for 491 days before dying on
July 9, 1850; the second Chief Executive to die in office.
His is the third shortest presidency in the history of the United States.

A landscape
hospitable in the extreme
is one definition of a garden.
Michael Pollan

Welcome to Fort Zachary Taylor Historic State Park

A garden gate
made of
light and shadow --
this is not at all
what you expect from a
south Florida beach.
For one thing, the air is
ridiculously cool.

The light
isn't slamming down on
you at full speed, the
way it usually does in the
Sunshine State --
here, it dithers,
hesitates in mid-air,
gives you time
to consider those aspects of
illumination that are more open
to interpretation.

And that purling rustle
in the canopy above --
what *is* that sound?

Oh, right.
That's the sound of you,
eavesdropping
on the universe.

Welcome to the Garden of the Whispering Pines.

Truth is, the Whispering Pines are not actually pines. They are in fact deciduous trees with coniferous characteristics that give them every *appearance* of a pine: the needle-like leaves, the turpentine scent, the pine cones.

Truth is that the habitat here, a serene and unspoiled timberland, is actually a landscape as contrived as any Baroque parterre.

Truth is that the Whispering Pine is more correctly known as the **Australian Pine** and, simply because of that, there are legions of native plant people who can't stand this tree and are determined to destroy every last one of them in the state of Florida.

Introducing the Australian Pine
Casuarina equisetifolia

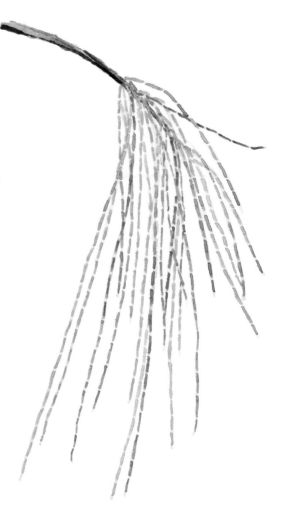

The slender, wispy "needles" of the Australian Pine are actually branchlets, each approx. 8 inches (20 cm.) long, each supporting infinitesimally small leaves. The fruit of the Australian Pine has the exact appearance of a pine cone, except that it is inordinately tiny, about one inch (24 mm) long.

In its native habitat in Australia, the tree is found along the coastline of the Tasmanian Sea and on the beaches of the Northern Territory.

Casuarina wood is exceptionally hard and has long been favored by the Aboriginal people of Australia as their preferred material for making spears, digging sticks, and boomerangs.

The Australian Pine arrived on these shores back when Florida was a swampland in dire need of theme parks and shopping centers. When it was discovered that the trees thrived in the salinity of Florida's water table, a consortium of developers and government officials imported millions of Australian Pines to Florida, and planted them in specially made forests to stabilize and beautify thousands of mucky acres. The result was the Sunshine State's land booms of the 1920s and the 1950s, in which real estate tycoons made a killing.

And then, out of the blue, after decades of service to the bureaucrats and speculators of Florida, in 1997 the noble Australian Pine was declared an *invasive species* and an enemy of the state.

Section 369.252, Florida Statutes, prohibits the possession, collection, transportation, cultivation, and importation of the Australian Pine as a Category 1 (worst of the worst) invasive species.

This outlawing of the Australian Pine was a triumph for parochial government botanists and do-gooder Native Plant Societies. Together they vowed to chop down every last Australian Pine, from the Everglades to the Georgia border.

Their big mistake came when they set their sights on the forest at Fort Zach Beach.

**In Key West
nobody gets away with calling the
Whispering Pine an *invasive species*.**

A coalition of local artists and politicians, armed with overwhelming public support, banded together to save the pines on Fort Zach Beach. All over Key West SAVE OUR PINES became the rallying cry at many a public protest, many a civil court action, and many, many, many a cocktail hour.

And thus began the fight for the life and death of the Key West Australian Pine forest that came to be known as

The Battle of the Tree Huggers.

Because

* In a hot, dry, and exposed recreation area, the Australian Pines at Fort Zach beach offer the charming simulacrum of a cool New England woodland.

* The Australian Pines tower over the surrounding cultivation, and their presence in the Key West landscape is a distinctive landmark signifying **home**.

* Fort Zach Beach is made entirely of landfill. It is the dumping ground of a 1967 dredging project that deepened a nearby harbor so it could accommodate nuclear submarines. Thusly, being that the beach was manufactured from stuff that was shoveled up from the bottom of the sea, there has *never* been any kind of "native" horticulture here in the first place for the Australian Pines to dispossess.

* The forest at Fort Zach Beach makes up the largest green space on Key West.

SAVE OUR PINES   SAVE OUR PINES   SAVE OUR PINES

* Florida bureaucrats don't hate *all* Australian pines, just THE Australian Pine.
They *love* the Wollemi Pine, an Australian pine that became world famous in 1994 when
a hiker came across a small group of them growing in a remote wilderness area Down
Under. Previously, the pine had been classified as extinct, so this finding became the
horticultural event of the year as the discovery of a 200-million year-old "living fossil."

When scientists cataloged fewer than 100 Wollemi Pines extant in the wild,
propagation became a priority. Seedlings of the rare tree were dispersed from Australia
to botanical gardens around the globe.

Guess where the largest number of Wollemi Pines are currently being cultivated.

Yes, IN FLORIDA! There are over 20,000 Australian Wollemi Pines growing
in nurseries around the state, on sale for about $100 each as a home garden curio.
And somehow, all of this Australian Wollemi Pine importation is OK with native plant
societies and the Florida Department of Agriculture.

* After decades of tireless service to the grateful citizens of the Conch Republic, the
Australian Pines of Key West have *earned* indigenous status.

This Is Called NOT SEEING THE FOREST FOR THE TREES.

The Australian Pine is a member of a family of flowering plants that is so old, it dates back half a billion years, to the great southern super-continent called Gondwana. Gondwana was a lush land teeming with dinosaurs and a certain small, furry-tailed, rat-like creature that came to be rather important to the development of the species called *Homo sapiens*.

Roughly 200 million years ago the super-continent Gondwana broke up into the fragments that we now know as South America, Africa, India, Madagascar, and Antarctica.

Before it completed its slow slide towards the South Pole, Antarctica shed its eastern region while it was still stocked with the original tropical biome of the old Gondwana. This breakaway slab moseyed northward and is currently occupying a rather large bit of the Tropic of Capricorn. We call it Australia. Along for the ride on this floating remnant of the Antarctic jungle were the direct ancestors of the Australian Pines now growing on the beach at Fort Zach in Key West.

Now, those Whispering Pines would have been perfectly happy to stay put Down Under, but the real estate developers of Florida had other plans. And now our dear Whispering Australian Pines are scheduled for annihilation simply because they lack a North American pedigree.

I want you take a moment to sit in the shade of these fine trees here on Fort Zach Beach. Let yourself merge with every leafy ripple of air, every flickering shadow, every whiff of terpene from the Australian Pines. Let the bedimming of the present take you back, back, back; back to the protohuman consciousness arising on Gondwana.

Inhale: You *are* that small rat-like mammal scurrying across the sand. You *are* the warm-blooded bound-for-domination rodent-like mammal that out-lasted the huge, bound-for-extinction Cryolophosaurus that walked like thunder across the land.

Exhale: You *are* the primeval, the survivor, the ancestor. You *are* the first flicker of *us*.

So as you see, this is not a silly turf war over what seems to be the absurdly small stakes of a few shade trees on a patch of beach at the edge of town.

This is a battle to preserve the sight, sound, and smells of the primordial Gondwana forest, the place where we can still experience the terrestrial origins of our very existence.

That's what makes the Australian Whispering Pines worth fighting for.

CANARY
ISLAND
DATE
PALM

native of the
Canary Islands

CAT PALM
native of
Southeast Mexico

SATAKI PALM
native of
Ryukyu Island, Japan

BAMBOO
native of Indochina

Let's see how many of Florida's favorite trees
DO NOT COME FROM FLORIDA

PUERTO RICAN
HAT PALM
native of
P.R. & Hispaniola

PEREGRINA
from Cuba

CHRISTMAS PALM
native of the
Philippines & Malaysia

FRANGIPANI
native to Central America & the Amazon

PINK POWDERPUFF
from Suriname

BETEL PALM
native of
Southeast Asia

OIL PALM
native of West & Central Africa

GEBANG PALM
native from NE India to York Peninsula, Australia

Why Native Plant Societies Are Barking Up the Wrong Tree

CARPENTARIA
PALM
*native of
Australia*

BISMARK PALM
native of West & North Madagascar

DESERT FAN PALM
*native of
California*

Michael Pollan, who does NOT compare native plant societies to Nazis, has this to say about the ideology of native plant societies:

> ...under National Socialism, the mania for natural gardening and native plants became government policy. A team working under Heinrich Himmler set forth "Rules of the Design of the Landscape" which stipulated a "close-to-nature" style and the exclusive use of native plants. Specific alien species were marked for elimination. In 1942, a team of Saxon botanists working for the Central Office of Vegetative Mapping embarked on "a war of extermination" against *Impatiens parviflora*, a small woodland flower regarded as an alien.
>
> **Against Nativism,**
> *The New York Times Magazine,*
> May 15, 1994

James Barilla, in **Gardening for Climate Change**, *The New York Times*, May 3, 2014:

> It doesn't make sense to think in terms of native and nonnative ... One study conducted in Davis Calif. found that 29 of 32 native butterflies in that city breed on nonnative plants. Thirteen of those butterflies have no native host plants; they persist because nonnative plants support them ... gardening means making the yard hospitable to as many species as possible without worrying so much about whether they originally belonged there or not.

Emma Maris,
The Rambunctious Garden:

The label *invasive species* is recent, stretching
back a couple of decades, but human
introduction stretches back into pre-history. . .
Humans are sentimental creatures. When
moving from one part of the world to
another we have a history of toting with us
garden plants and pets, game birds and game
fish, even songbirds to cheer us up ...
spending time and money battling exotics
simply because they are not "supposed" be
where they are drains time and money away
from more constructive projects.

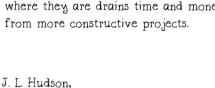

BANYAN
from India

J. L. Hudson,
The Ethnobotanical Catalog of Seeds:

There is an idea, popular in some circles, that "non-native"
species are somehow harmful, that "aggressive exotics" can
invade ecosystems and destroy "native species". ... I would
like to point out that there is absolutely no biological validity
to the concepts of "native" and "exotic" species, nor is there
evidence that man's introduction of species into new habitats
has any negative impact on global biological diversity. On the
contrary, the aid we have given species in their movement
around the world has served to increase both global and local
diversity. It is one of the few human activities which is
beneficial to the non-human creation. It cannot be
distinguished from the movement of species by wind or ocean
currents, or the aid other species give to their fellows, such as
the distribution of seeds by migrating birds.

LOQUAT
native of
China

Final victory in the Battle of the Tree Huggers was achieved on March 19, 2008, with the signing of a Memorandum of Understanding from the Florida Department of Environmental Protection. It immediately and permanently halted the removal of the Australian Pines at Fort Zach Beach.

As the Florida State Task Force studying the situation in Key West concluded: **In some cases exotic vegetation is allowed to remain because it is historically accurate and contributes to the character of a cultural landscape.**

This memorandum affected only the 900 pines at Fort Zach Beach, leaving vulnerable the three hundred million acres of pineland in the rest of Florida. However, inspired by the success of the Save Our Pines campaign in Key West, other Australian Pine preservation societies have suited up for battle, intent on saving the Sunshine State from itself, one Whispering Pine at a time.

In 2015 Mayor Craig Cates of the City of Key West, State of Florida, proclaimed the third Sunday of March to be henceforth celebrated as SAVE OUR PINES DAY.

Key West Gardening Tip:
No Snivelling

The idea for the most famous poem about Key West came to Wallace Stevens in the Winter of 1934. The story goes that Stevens, in town for his annual bender, was walking off a hangover on the Casa Marina beach one morning when he came upon a woman singing to the ocean. She inspired an epiphany about the meaning of life and art that Stevens tried to explain in a poem he called *The Idea of Order at Key West*, which is actually not much about Key West at all.

She sang beyond the genius of the sea is the first line of the poem and that, at least, has a little something to do with Key West. *The genius of the sea* is as good an explanation as any as to what brings people to this island of outlaws in the Gulf of Mexico.

O.K., some people might come to Key West just to see how long they can live on nothing but daiquiris and key lime pie. But the many others who are drawn here spend days and sunsets on the waterfront, mesmerized by the endless waves, breaking in time to the infinite heartbeat of . . what?

It's a mystery.

I, for one, am happy to be here, on Fort Zach beach, in close contact with the great enigmas of life. The homey scent of the Australian Pines, the light of a westward-ho sun, the slow-going breeze that warms the shadows, all reminders of the older-than-ancient tropical forests of Antarctica. It's both very strange and very familiar.

I lapse into contented thoughts about the order of things in Key West, and of the immense continuity of the life force of Planet Earth. I'm happy to be alive. I'm happy that there is no one singing anywhere near me. People can be so annoying.

The soul of a garden comprises seasons, epochs, eons ... while we humans can barely hold on to ten minutes at a time. It takes this, the slowest of garden experiences, to make us profoundly aware of our moment in the hierarchy of eternity.

To the citizens of the Conch Republic who came together to pitch the long and atrocious bureaucratic battle to keep intact this strange, atavistic Be-In, here in the Australian Pine forest on the beach at Fort Zach, I give my utmost gratitude and admiration.

There's not a sniveller among you.

Marrakech

Weekend in the Oasis

Don't you love the sound of *a weekend in Marrakech*? Doesn't it sounds so depraved, and dapper? In other words so *me*?

Having already been to Casablanca and Rabat in my 20s, I'd long considered Morocco *done*. Then a gardener friend told me about the **Jardin Majorelle** in Marrakech. It's one of the Top Ten connoisseur gardens in the world. The *world*!

And I'd never heard of it.

Then I remembered my unfulfilled wish to partake of an authentic Moroccan tea experience. Ahhh... tea. As much as gardens and travel, I love tea.

So now I had plenty of reasons (two) to book a flight to Marrakech.

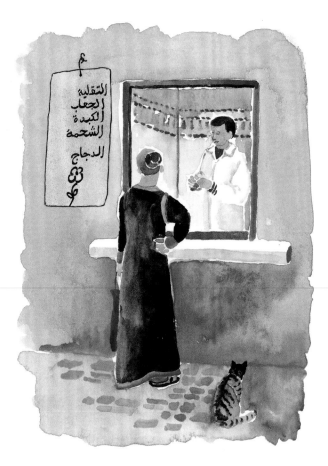

In Marrakech, Arabian open-heartedness is served up with a generous dose of pan-African mysticism, a dollop of French *savoir-vivre*, and a garnish of Moorish grace. The vibe is irresistible to meaning-of-life seekers and international hipsters looking for a scene.

Now, about the tea:

Tea drinking is the most prevalent custom of daily life in Morocco. The kingdom has the highest per-capita consumption of tea in the world -- an average of four cups a day. This makes Morocco unique among Arab nations, where coffee is by far the predominate beverage. It's that fondness for tea that makes Morocco a nation of outstanding hospitality.

Life is not easy in the Maghreb. So there is tea. Hardship makes courtesy a prime virtue, so there is tea. Moments of joy must be shared and celebrated, so there is tea. Visitors must be welcomed, business must be bargained, stories must be told, souls must be soothed.

There is always tea.

I arrived in Marrakech on an afternoon flight from Paris.
It had been ages since my last trip to North Africa and the culture
shock was coming on strong. I needed a cup of tea *pronto*.

Fatima, gracious tea-maker of the *Riad les Orangers d'Alilia*, spoons a measure of gunpowder tea into a pot.

She adds freshly wilted spearmint leaves, and fills the pot with boiling water.

The tea steeps.

Minutes pass.

The riad's inner courtyard has neither doors nor windows to the outside world -- this is called *the architecture of the veil*. However, every surface is illuminated by the clear desert light shining in from the open roof high above.

A fountain splashes into a turquoise pool. Small brown birds, *house buntings*, perch in the orange trees and chirp for crumbs of *fekka*.

Fatima stirs spoonsful of sugar into the kettle and relights the flame for a second boil.

Her expert sense of tea will tell her when it's time to pour.

I am at home in this, the glorious unhurried purposefulness of the moment.

TEA TIME *in the* KASBAH

Every cup of tea is an oasis, a private retreat to the place in your soul where you feel calm, content, and cared for. It's the Moroccan genius to have created an entire desert culture around tea, around these small every day moments of oasis.

I (Peace Corps Niger 1980 - 1982) couldn't spend a weekend in Marrakech without checking in with a local Peace Corps Volunteer. That's how I met Sarah Quinn, PCV from Georgia, who had been working in Morocco for two years as the program director for a Women and Arts Development project. She invited me to visit her village in the foothills of the Atlas Mountains, a mere 13 mile (22 kilometer), one-hour bus ride from Marrakech, to meet the artists of the local women's crafts cooperative.

The gracious Madame Zenib, president of *Creation Tameslouht*, welcomed us to her home and made us comfortable in her enormous salon. She had piles of beautiful traditional embroideries to show me, and an inventory of items made especially for the export market. The tastes of tourists seemed to amuse her. (Well, haven't you wondered why an adult person would want to own a Disney World T-shirt?) She told stories about her work as an entrepreneur artist and how her arts cooperative gives its members the opportunity to grow their skills and earn some personal independence. We also talked about cats -- and that's not the best part.

Tea was served.

The Arabian Nights/ Rive Gauche Garden Gate to Le Jardin Majorelle

The Jardin Majorelle is a small walled garden within the sprawling estate belonging to the famous French couturier Yves Saint Laurent and his partner, Pierre Bergé. When YSL and M. Bergé purchased the 10-acre property in 1980 its 2 ½-acre (10,000 sq. m.) garden had gone to seed, although it was still well known in Marrakech as a local curiosity, the handiwork of an eccentric, French-born artist called **Jacques Majorelle** (1886 - 1962).

The young Jacques Majorelle left his home in Nancy in 1919, seeking artistic inspiration in the exotic Orient, which was a very trendy thing to do among young bohemians at the time. In Marrakech he found a quality of light and color that made it pointless for him to paint anywhere else.

His vibrant landscape and genre paintings of the Maghreb sold well in Paris, until gardening took over his life. That happened when Majorelle was 40 years old and he acquired this estate and became a full-time gardener.

Majorelle always said that his gardening obsession would be the death of him, as his maniacal plant collecting brought him to the brink of bankruptcy. But, in the end, it was a car crash that did him in. Jacques Majorelle died in 1962 at the age of seventy-six.

When Yves Saint Laurent and Pierre Bergé first laid eyes on the Majorelle estate, it was scheduled for destruction in order to make way for a luxury hotel. After their purchase of the place, YSL and M. Bergé spent a decade restoring Jacques Majorelle's magnificent garden, which they maintained as their private oasis until 2001, when it was opened it to the public.

Almost immediately, the Jardin Majorelle became famous as a must-see garden. Its many thousands of international visitors make it one of the top tourist attractions in all of North Africa.

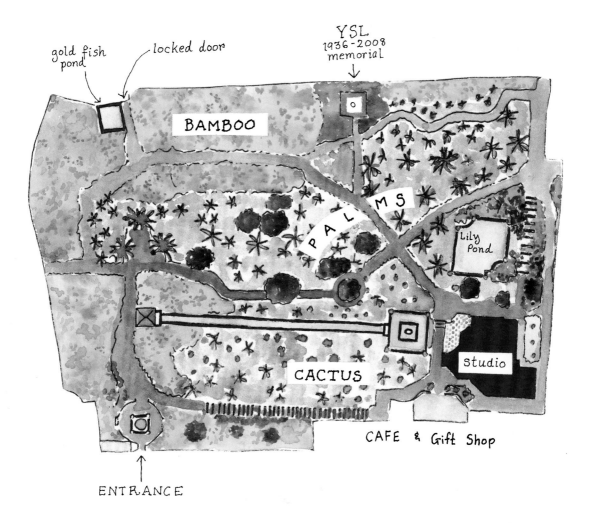

gold fish pond

locked door

YSL
1936-2008
memorial

BAMBOO

PALMS

Lily Pond

CACTUS

studio

ENTRANCE

CAFE & Gift Shop

The Jardin Majorelle contains three distinct installations: a bamboo grove, a palm tree arboretum, and a cactus xeriscape. In restoring Jacques Majorelle's greatest work of art, Yves Saint Laurent and Pierre Bergé continued Majorelle's ambitious plantings and the garden is now home to more than 300 species of plants from five continents. Many of their plants are rare or endangered, or both, such as the *Hedyscepe canterburyana* palm tree from Lord Howe Island.

Before I visited the garden I had no idea that Lord Howe Island was a real place. But now I know that Lord Howe Island is a tiny speck of lava off the coast of Australia, and it has four endemic palms -- all threatened by loss of habitat -- and the beautiful *H. canterburyana* palm tree is the most rare of the lot.

Thank you, Jardin Majorelle.

It's not what you think.

Yes, it's a bamboo grove.

No, it's not Zen.

Shade is a luxury here on the North Saharan steppe and, since this garden is all about luxury, the Majorelle garden experience begins with a plunge into a deep, dark, luxuriant pool of shade.

Although bamboo is not usually associated with Africa, Montane Bamboo happens to thrive in the eastern and central African highlands. This native evergreen actually makes up 4% of the continent's forest cover.

So, stepping into the bamboo grove of the Jardin Majorelle is like wading into the cool air of an Afro-Alpine forest.

Yes, it gets *that* blue here in the Jardin Majorelle.

In fact, it gets *extremely* blue.

Morocco is renowned for a lavish use of the color blue in its folk arts and crafts so, naturally, Jacques Majorelle had to include this local color in his garden. But first he had to electrify it, blast the folksiness out of it.

After many years of effort he achieved an intensely saturated hue that he trademarked as **Majorelle Bleu.**

Sadly, its formula was a secret that Majorelle took with him to his grave.

To reproduce the bluer-than-blue color scheme in the *jardin* I had to source paint from Switzerland, from a firm that sells an almost Majorelle Bleu, called

Ultramarinblau,

for $45.00 per cup.

That's not cheap.

Ounce for ounce, this Majorelle Bleu is as pricey as a bottle of Moët & Chandon Dom Perignon.

A Paradise Garden
for the Avant-Garde

A water feature is essential to the core meaning of gardens in Islamic desert lands, where water is a God-given miracle. To exalt the glory of this gift, every Islamic garden is made in the likeness of God's Paradise as described in the Koran -- a lush paradise watered by flowing rivers.

A traditional **Paradise Garden** has, at its center, two artificial water channels, intersecting at right angles, symbolizing the rivers of heaven.

One of the most lavish such Paradise Garden is a 55-acre affair in Uttar Pradesh, a relic of India's Islamic Moghul Empire. Unfortunately, the garden has been entirely over-shadowed by an architectural feature at one end of it, called the Taj Mahal.

Jacques Majorelle, ever the non-conformist, installed just a single stand-alone water channel in his garden, terminating at a large pool with a fountain in the center of it. I think of his linear water feature as his modernist homage to the Islamic gardening protocols of his dearly beloved adopted homeland.

As for his Taj Mahal, Majorelle built, in 1931, a villa-studio in the brutally intellectual principles of Cubism. A decade later, he installed a decorative triple-arched trellis over the front porch, a feature that purists say destroys the integrity of the Cubist structure.

I am of the opinion that this little flourish of filigree became necessary to Majorelle's peace of mind. Judging by his garden, Majorelle loved the jumble and sensuality of dense, sinuous vegetation, and I think that when he built this hard-edged edifice he seriously misjudged the long-term appeal of living with strict, straight-edged, analytical formalism.

So he put a big green doo-dad on it and lived happily ever after.

The Jardin Majorelle is an extremely busy space, crammed with plants and structures and textures and color. Yet a sense of calm and order prevails throughout the grounds. In spite of its mix of desert, tropical, and *montagne* plantings, the Jardin Majorelle is an extraordinarily *coherent* garden.

Well, of course. With YSL and M. Bergé as its curators, the garden experience here is steeped in the same impeccable chic of a YSL runway collection, the same sexy exoticism made elegant by the immaculate craftsmanship of its fabrication. And there is this, which is an aspect that I sense everywhere in the Majorelle: This was a well-loved garden that loved its gardeners back.

I Can't Resist a Keep Out Sign or Even An Insinuation of It

I'd been strolling the grounds for over an hour. I had checked out the garden's café, but could see that it was just a place to quench your thirst and nothing more.

I wasn't ready to quit the soothing civility of the Majorelle for the bustle of Marrakech, so I headed back into the cathedral-like bamboo grove. I soon found myself on a path that I had not noticed before.

At the end of the path, hidden in a remote corner of the garden, there was a goldfish pond and a big blue door. It was locked.

I knew immediately that the big blue door had to be the main access to the Jardin Majorelle **from the other side.**

The *other side* is strictly off limits to the public. The *other side* is YSL's very private home base, the place where, throughout the 1980s, he hosted huge parties for his famous international jet-setting friends who flocked to The Red City for the sumptuously decadent vibe of Marrakech in the 1980s.

The guesthouse behind this wall is called the **Dar es Saada**, *House of Happiness.* The main house is the **Villa Oasis.**

An oasis in Marrakech was a necessity for Yves Saint Laurent, a troubled soul described by his partner Pierre Bergé as having been "born with a nervous breakdown." YSL was uneasy with his fame, and was frequently exhausted by his obligation to constantly create goods for his international fashion and lifestyle empire. When he needed to escape from the pressures of business it was here, to his Villa Oasis, that YSL retreated. In Marrakech YSL could find his inner peace and revive the genius that made him the preeminent creator of *la mode* in the last half of the 20th century.

When Yves Saint Laurent died in 2008, his ashes were scattered in the Jardin Majorelle. Not far from this big blue locked door, a small plinth stands on the public side of the wall, as a memorial to the love the YSL had for Marrakech.

I shimmied up this big blue locked door (the door's panels make excellent footholds) and got a peep at the *other side.* I didn't see much, just the roof line of the inner sanctum.

I also got a glimpse of the tower of the Villa Oasis, in which I hope is a room that, if it does exist, must be the perfect place to sit and view the world while sipping a cup of Moroccan mint tea.

Marrakech Gardening Tip:
Oasis isn't a place. It's a stretch of the imagination.

I like gardens that have a point of view. I like them so much that it is worth it to me to travel thousands of miles to experience a garden with a one-of-a-kind point of view.

Which brings me to the Jardin Majorelle.

There is no doubt that this garden has a powerful point of view. The question is: *Whose?*

* Jacques Majorelle envisioned the garden.
* But Yves Saint Laurent is responsible for its existence.
* The fact that the garden is still known as the *Majorelle* must mean that it's *his* esthetics that prevail in this garden experience.
* But it is YSL's perfectionism and taste, as a great designer and Savant of the Vibe that permeates every aspect of the garden's presentation.

I've thought about this for a long time, over many cups of tea. And I've come to the conclusion that, regarding the question as to whose point of view is on display in the Jardin Majorelle, the answer has to be: **Genius.**

Genius is the whole story of this garden.

* Majorelle had the genius to conceive such a garden as this, both intellectual and voluptuous; and then he integrated his vision with the surrounding French, African, and Arabian cultural mish-mash, despite its being so *completely* out of context.
* Yves Saint Laurent had the genius to see past the deterioration of the neglected Majorelle property and perceive the soul, the intention, and the purpose of Majorelle's garden.

YSL's supernatural attunement to Majorelle, and his total success in perpetuating the unique gardening concepts of a man he never met, and then turning this rapport into his own unique oasis, constitutes genius, in my book. This book, in fact. The one you're reading right now.

The psychic collaboration between Yves Saint Laurent and Jacques Majorelle, and the personal collaboration between YSL and Pierre Bergé, is evident in the emotional resonance and tranquilty of this garden experience. And that's what gives this place a genius all its own.

New
Orleans
Rose Garden Voodoo

America has only three cities:
New York, San Francisco, &
New Orleans
Everywhere else is Cleveland.
Tennessee Williams

Living in New Orleans means something soulful and strange and ludicrous that living in Edinburgh or Long Island does not.

Because in oh, so many ways, life in New Orleans is completely impossible. If it's not the crazy heat and the 80% humidity; or the fact that New Orleans is a below sea-level city surrounded by six hundred square miles of Lake Pontchartrain on one side, and a half-million acres of the swampy Mississippi River Delta on the other; or that NOLA continues to sink at the rate of 1/5 inch (0.5 centimeter) per year, then it's the hurricanes that will do you in.

No one sane would live here, says Karen.
That's Karen Kersting, who has lived and gardened in New Orleans for 30 years. New Orleans, she says, is only for those demented few whose zest for life comes from tempting fate, which in local parlance is called *Laissez les bons temps rouler.* Yes, that's French, which is another thing about New Orleans that makes it so different from Cleveland. (Sorry, Cleveland.)
Anyhoo. I'm here in the Crescent City because I love roses, and Karen Kersting has a spectacular rose garden in the 14th Ward, Uptown. A visit to my favorite American city to see my favorite flower is what I call *Letting the good times roll.*

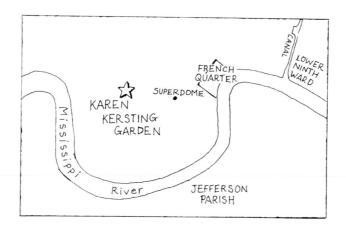

When Hurricane Katrina headed towards New Orleans in August of 2005, Karen evacuated ahead of the storm to Houston. She returned home to find her house flooded with seven feet of water. Karen's neighbor took one look at the devastation and took off to find a more ordinary life *anywhere else*.

But Karen, after three decades of living in New Orleans, has developed a strong aversion to *ordinary*. So she doubled-down: She bought that neighbor's house, razed it, and turned the vacant lot into extra gardening space.

It took her six years to restore her 1920s Arts and Crafts cottage.

And then she declared final victory over Hurricane Katrina by planting a rose garden.

The gate says it all. It's French, vintage, probably circa 1900, when artisans in Normandy could get away with putting Art Nouveau flourishes on traditional woodworking. But more importantly, this garden gate is a **Katrinket**.

I learned from Karen that a Katrinket is the ridiculously expensive, indulgent, and therapeutic thing that people bought whilst in the throes of digging out of the muck and misery of Hurricane Katrina. Usually it's something like an Hermès handbag, or a Harley. Something that says *Let the good times roll* once again.

For Karen it was this one-and-only antique Art Nouveau French French Provincial Good Time Rolling Garden Gate.

69

Of All the Ways a Garden Can Come into Being
This Is My Favorite

In the aftermath of Hurricane Katrina, Karen lived in her driveway for an entire year in a trailer so tiny that even her Chihuahua got claustrophobia. If you had to live in *your* driveway for a year, you *too* would come to loathe the sight of it. So, as soon as she gave FEMA back their trailer, Karen planted its old parking space with twelve kinds of roses. Exactly twelve.

    Because, Karen says, *what lady doesn't deserve a dozen roses?*

The Rambling Rose
vanilla, amber, parchment

Miss Gertrude Jekyll
sweet — sugary & creamy

Tropicana carnations & ice

Milady Banks cut grass & violets
La Duchesse satin & licorice

Zephirine
old ballgowns and
late Spring

Geoff H.
  a love song

Pat Austin
  playful & happy

4th of July   the way the air smells
        after a thunderstorm

Peach Drift   bashful & naive —
        lilac powder & morning fog
The Metairie Rose
        lemonade and copper pennies
Scentsational
        soap, honey, &
            Summer nights

Scentsational

Karen's driveway, it turns out, is the ideal setting for a **scent garden**. The enclosed space traps the fragrances coming from each rose, and concentrates all the aromas into a heightened experience of the voodoo power of scent.

You know that voodoo power if you are made melancholy by the scent of pear blossoms, or if you're overwhelmed with a sense of déjà vu by a whiff of night blooming jasmine. Sometimes you don't even know what hit you -- one minute you're fine, and the next you can't get *Nights in White Satin* out of your head ... look around. There's probably a Moody Blues trigger nearby.

Triggers: The scents we inhale go directly to the most primitive part of our brain, the **limbic system**. Picture your brain as a hard-boiled egg. The limbic system is the yolk. It's where our most primitive emotions and (some say, reptilian) instincts are stashed away, deep within the egg white of our more highly evolved and civilized cerebrum.

Scent has this direct line to the limbic system because our sense of smell is, along with taste (think of the voodoo of Proust's *madeleine*) the most primitive of the senses. Before our senses of sight, hearing, or touch evolved, there was a nearsighted, hard of hearing, cold-blooded predator called *cynognuthus* that sniffed a *glossopteris* and went *Ahhhh ... that brings back fond memories of Autumn*. That would have been 235 million Autumns ago and, by the way, that *cynognuthus* is most likely the reptile in charge of the basic instincts that we have stashed in the depths of our limbic system.

And so it is that **scent** penetrates our veneer of rationality and triggers a memory in the limbic system that can either feel like a sock in the guts or a free fall through heaven.

A single scent can contain up to 50 different components. A master *parfumier*, the supreme architect of smells, has the skill to de-code that complexity and restructure it in blends that bring out the desired earthy and ethereal qualities when the selected scents cascade in sequence:

First, a light, heady flourish.

Next, an illustrious fullness.

Lastly, a lingering, potent finish.

In the trade, these are called the **Top**, **Middle**, and **Base** Notes.

Karen Kersting's
Twelve Rose Bouquet

Top Note: SURVIVAL
Terracotta, fern, bark, and cinnamon

Middle Note: CELEBRATION
Spice Island meadows and essence of myrrh

Base Note: SERENITY
Oakmoss, waterfalls,
and the champagne scent of white flowers

That which God said to the ROSE
and caused it to laugh in full-blown beauty

He said to my heart
and made it a hundred times more beautiful

RUMI Persian poet, 1207 - 1273

I went into the garden in the morning dusk
When sorrow enveloped me like a cloud
And the breeze brought to me
the scent of spices
As a healing balm for my ailing soul

Moses ben Jacob ibn Ezra (1060 - 1188)

Lagniappe

Lan-*yap* - noun; the New Orleans tradition of giving a surprising little something extra, as when the bartender at Tujague's fixes you a sazerac and gives you an extra shot of rye for your go cup.

It's Louisiana. Of course there's a gator in the lily pond. There are also azaleas, hydrangeas, amaryllis, and Chinese holly. There are dwarf indigos, bower vines, passionflowers, Sapphire showers, day lilies, and Gerbera daisies.

There's also bonsai: sweet bay, cypress, pecan, pine, and French bay leaf. There's a Night-Blooming Cereus!

In all, there are over 100 plants and 75 species in Karen's garden, not counting the vegetable garden and the citrus trees and the comings and goings of the annuals. Karen Kersting has *la main verte*.

My friend David, from New Orleans, tells me that the worst thing about the rest of America is that when you ask people from there, *How you doing?*, all they ever say is *Fine*.

Fine?? Where David comes from (the old Faubourg Lafayette of the 10th Ward), *Fine* would be an affront to civility, so major a *faux pas* that it borders on insult.

When the courteous people of New Orleans ask *How you doing?*, they expect, and gladly listen to, a detailed report of yourself and at least five other family members or mutual acquaintances. That's why front porches were invented. That's why, after I've had the tour of her garden, Karen and I settle down in the cool shade of her front porch to ask each other, *How you doing?*

We chat about the latest local scandals (always a hugely entertaining topic of conversation in New Orleans). Karen shows me a block of wood from the PT boat that she's helping to restore for the National World War II Museum on Magazine Street. She invites me to come back to New Orleans for Jazz Fest. Karen will be manning the Carrollton Rotary Club booth there, selling beer for charity.

You see what I mean? **Lagniappe**.

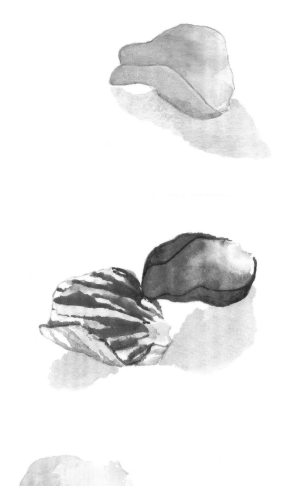

New Orleans Gardening Tip:
Tempt Fate

There's heat, history, rot, and superstition saturating the atmosphere of the Crescent City. In the air is the heavy scent of train smoke and Spanish moss; Catholic incense, char-grilled oysters, wood porches, and vetiver root.

And then there's the stench of Louisiana political corruption, blended in with the putrid odor of the utter incompetence of municipal government.

Sometimes, Karen tells me, *I wonder why I don't just give up and go live in my car with my dog.*

Of course she doesn't mean it. Yes, New Orleans makes almost no practical sense as a city. And yes, the people of New Orleans *know* this.

But they don't (for the most part) give up and go live in their cars. They don't (for the most part) call it quits and move to Cleveland. (Sorry, Cleveland.)

They dance at funerals and make impromptu parades all through Second Line Season. They keep the faith, whether it's in their everyday voodoo -- the slice of pound cake left for Saint Expedite on Rampart Street, the feather pillow floating down the Mississippi River -- or it's in the healing power of a good beignet. They lose it all and they rebuild; they endure and they celebrate.

You can't deny it. There's grandeur in the gist of everyday life in New Orleans.

Six months after I visited Karen and her garden, an especially cruel Winter killed her Bougainvillea down to the roots but, surprisingly, the roses fared well. The Zephirine Drouhin is still the Voodoo Queen of the garden, sending out a heavy damask scent that brings back memories of velvet and jewelry boxes, and is inspirited with all the benevolence of a Padua saint.

Forecasters predict a below-average storm season this year, which impacts life in the Crescent City only so far as it cuts down on the number of hurricane parties thrown.

Anyway, isn't surviving every day, even if you live in Cleveland, an event against all odds? We'd all be a lot happier if we rejoiced in our daily good fortune the way they do in New Orleans, where tempting fate is a way of life and Friday night waltzing at Tipitina's is as much a prayer as a prayer.

Long Island
Part One

Making a Japanese Garden
Feel at Home

BEACON TOWERS
a Gothic Fantasy built in 1918
for Alva Vanderbilt Belmont and was the model for the   castle in
The
Wizard
of
OZ

COE HALL 1921
Tudor Revival

409 acres
of gardens
designed by
**OLMSTED
BROTHERS**

CASTLE   GOULD
built   1912
in 12ᵗʰc. Anglo-   -Norman style

The Guggenheim **FALAISE**
built 1923 in Medieval
Norman French Eclectic style

My 80-year old neighbor tells me that back in her school days, back in the 1940s, the Old Money families of Long Island were *still* deeply offended by *The Great Gatsby*. In that book, F. Scott Fitzgerald had dared to make our neck of the woods look **tacky**.

You see, Jay Gatsby and those terrible people the Buchanans were made out to live on the North Shore of Long Island, and the North Shore has always held itself apart from -- and, I'll say it, *above* -- the rest of Long Island. That's why it's called the Gold Coast.

It all goes back to the Gilded Age, when the North Shore was where the millionaire bankers, lawyers, and industrialists of New York built their country castles. In those days, a 60-room pile of European architectural references was not deemed the least bit *tacky*.

F. Scott Fitzgerald estimated that it cost him $3,000 a month to maintain his residence on the North Shore while he wrote *The Great Gatsby*, in 1924. At the time, the average salary for a certified public accountant was a whopping $250 a month.

All this is context for the garden we are visiting in this chapter. Be assured that the garden is Old Money, and not at all tacky, but, in the best traditions of the Gold Coast, it is every bit the folly as any robber baron's pretend-Gothic castle.

Welcome to the
John P. Humes
Japanese Stroll Garden.

Your visit to the John P. Humes Japanese Stroll Garden will give you absolutely no sense of John P. Humes., Princeton Class of '43. So let me tell you that John P. Humes was the scion of a socially prominent Virginia family, partner in a Wall Street law firm, and the Nixon-appointed ambassador to Austria (1969 - 1975). In 1960, he and his wife, Jean Cooper Schmidlapp, M.D., heiress to an old Ohio banking fortune, journeyed to Japan, after which John P. Humes returned with a hankering to have his very own Japanese garden on Long Island. So Dr. Schmidlapp Hume turned over this 4-acre (16,000 sq. meter) corner of their backyard to him, and he let rip.

At the Corner of Oyster Bay Road and Dogwood Lane.

The John P. Humes Japanese Stroll Garden was opened to the public in 1986.

Since 1993 the garden has been under the management of The Garden Conservancy, a nonprofit organization headquartered in Cold Spring, New York, dedicated to the preservation of exceptional gardens for the public's enjoyment and education.

Every Garden Has a Point of View,
Especially a Japanese Garden in 1960s America

In 1960, the year that John P. Humes made his fateful trip to Japan, the country was just eight years removed from its occupation by U.S. military forces following World War II. But in the meantime, there had been a complete about-face in American popular culture regarding its former enemy. Japan was now very much in fashion, particularly among the economic elites who could afford air travel. Filling one's home with Japanese decorative arts was a way of showing off one's internationalism.

This fancy for Japanese novelties reached a peak in 1963, when a Japanese-language song became a Number One pop hit in America. It was given the nonsense name **Sukiyaki** because that was easier for Americans to pronounce than its *real* title, **Anoko-No Namae-Wa Nantenkana** (*I Will Walk Looking Up*).

The song tells the story of a man, haunted by regret and misery, who walks while looking up at the sky so his tears won't fall down his cheeks. The melancholy of the music (there's even some mournful whistling) sounded to its American audience like a classic break-up song … but in actuality, the song was about the lyricist's anguish over the signing of the Treaty of Mutual Cooperation Between the United States and Japan. Among Japanese Nationalists, America was very much *out* of fashion.

In my opinion, Japanese gardens in America translate about as well as Japanese pop songs. In other words: very, very poorly. For proof I give you the John P. Humes Japanese Stroll Garden.

Although the space calls itself a **stroll garden**, a four-acre stroll garden such as this simply does not exist in Japan. Stroll gardens in Japan are set in ten to twenty acres of contrived scenery, and offer garden visitors miles and miles of pathways to give them the illusion of journeying to far-away places as they stroll along. Furthermore, the tea house, the Pond and Hill landscaping, and the Zen elements that are thrown into the experience of the John P. Humes Japanese garden don't make any sense *at all* in the context of a *stroll garden*.

Welcome to Mr. Humes's Folly.

These woods of Long Island
are no different in make-up, mood, and spirit
than any forest on Honshu.

Any Japanese visitor to the John P. Humes Japanese Stroll Garden would feel very much at home in the shapes and shadows of the garden's trees and plants. That's because Japan and the northeastern United States have over one hundred species of trees and flowering plants in common, despite the two regions being 6,758 miles (10,876 kms) apart.

For centuries this odd *discontinuous distribution* had nagged the scientific community as one of the great horticultural mysteries. The mystery was solved in 1912, when a young geophysicist, named Alfred Wegener, took a look at a map of the Earth and noticed that the land masses might fit neatly together if the planet was reassembled in the manner of a picture puzzle.

And that's how Albert Wegener discovered **Continental Drift**.

North America, Europe, and Asia were once interlocked as a single super-continent called Laurasia. Laurasia came apart about 200 million years ago and as its assorted bits drifted to their current locations, new biomes formed on the now-isolated continents. Much of the original Laurasian ecology disappeared...except in the two places on Earth where the climate and the topography were just right for its preservation: the islands of Japan and the northeastern coast of the United States.

Over millions of years of separation, small differences in the Japanese and American context called for little tweaks to be made to their common botanical inheritance.

For example, the American Dogwood tree produces a small red berry, suitable to the digestive tracts of the 90 species of New World birds that eat and disperse the seeds within the berry. The Japanese Dogwood, on the other hand, had a whole different set of circumstances to deal with so, instead of producing a small hard berry for birds, it evolved something entirely different, a fat juicy fruit to tempt its native disseminators: Snow Monkeys.

American Jack-in-the-pulpit
Arisaema triphyllum

Japanese
Jack-in-the-pulpit
also called Cobra Lily
Arisaema ringens

American Lady Fern
Athyrium felix-femina

Japanese
Painted Fern
Athyrium nipponicum 'Pictum'

American Sweetspire
Itea virginiana

Japanese
Sweetspire
Itea japonica

American blue flag iris
Iris versicolor

Japanese Iris
Iris kaempferi

The river has long
ceased to roar
but I still hear
the echo of its name

Anonymous, Late Heian period, c.1100

Zen Dry River

At the Bed of Moss Let Us Pause to Savor the Impending Nothingness That Dooms Every Atom in the Universe.

The most noble function of Japanese art is to express the melancholy of mortality and the inevitable decay of beauty, to act as a catalyst for the experience of sublime sorrow.
This mindfulness is found in every aspect of Japanese culture, in pottery, pop songs, haiku, and even in the way of tea.
When it comes to achieving that desired quality of existential desolation in a Japanese garden, it's moss that gets the job done.

There's Nothing Like It
in All of Oyster Bay

So now we've come to the centerpiece of the
John P. Hume Japanese Stroll Garden.

The tea house.

The two hundred maneuvers it takes to make
and serve a bowl of **matcha** tea have been
codified for centuries. In the art of gardening,
equally finicky rules have been codified by
the **Sakuteiki**, written c. 900 CE.

Regarded as the gardening bible of Japan, the
Sakuteiki is the source of 183 commandments for
the proper setting of stones and the appropriate
placement of streams, islands, trees, and
waterfalls in order to achieve the correct **fusui**
(feng shui) of the garden spirits.

Here is where I must confess that the one kind of tea I can't drink is *matcha* tea, and I
don't much care for Japanese gardens either. All that over-thinking ruins two of life's most
personal and ecstatic experiences, in my opinion. I believe that people should drink tea
with abandon, and make gardens that are true to their own vision of the world.

Which is why I make an exception to my general dislike of Japanese gardens for the one
and only John P. Humes Japanese Stroll Garden.

A *bijoux* Stroll Garden with bogus Zen-garden references and
a misbegotten quasi-Tea Garden set in a New World
Laurasian-esque woodland. I love this garden for being the
marvelous, wacky, and earnest apparition of a Japanese
garden experience that exists only in the mind and heart of
John Portner Humes.
This garden is one fine folly.

The John P. Humes Gardening Tip:
It's Never Too Late to Commit a Fine Folly

He who lives without folly is not so wise as he thinks.

Francois de La Rochefoucauld

He must have a little bit of folly who does not want to have more stupidity.

Michel de Montaigne

I always prefer the enthusiasm of a passionate folly to the indifference of wisdom.

Anatole France

When I call Mr. Humes's garden a **folly** I mean it with the greatest respect. I deeply admire the clarity and eccentricity of Mr. Humes' garden vision, and the tenacity and refinement of his actualization of it.

John P. Humes was 39 years old when he returned from his fateful trip to Japan. Back in 1960, that put him on the brink of middle age, when a man is most ripe for folly.

Folly holds a distinguished place in the Way of Gardening. In 1741 the 2nd Earl Temple commissioned Capability Brown to rip up the grounds of his Buckinghamshire estate to plant a carefully designed English landscape garden *in the English landscape.*

Francois Racine de Monville (1734 - 1791), a well known ladies' man, created a 99-acre Anglo-Asian-Ottoman garden park near Paris simply to have a way to entice women to take long, private walks with him.

The Hon. Charles Hamilton (1704 - 1786) of Surrey famously hired a hermit to live in his garden. The contract required the hermit to go barefoot, never cut his hair, wear a raggedy woolen robe, and never speak to visitors.

A colonel who served under the Duke of Wellington planted his garden with hundreds of oak trees in the formation of the charge of British heavy cavalry at the Battle of Waterloo.

In 2000, the mayor of Kitagawa (pop. 1,500) opened the *Jardin de Monet,* a weirdly meticulous reproduction of Giverny, in the rainy mountains of Kochi prefecture. It has since become one of the most popular tourist attractions in all of southern Japan.

In 2009, the Pothole Gardener of London, Steve Wheen, started a world-wide movement to create "unexpected moments of happiness" by making miniscule gardens in surprising public places such as, well, potholes.

Hr. Humes's neighbors, the Coes, who lived half a mile up the road, filled their 400-acre property with an Italian garden, a beech copse, a dwarf conifer collection, a rhododendron collection, a collection of 100 species of holly from around the world, and a "synoptic" garden of 500 trees planted alphabetically.

Mr. Humes's Japanese Stroll Garden folly is in fine company.

Long Island

Part Two

A Poet's Orchard in Autumn

The Village of Roslyn,
Gold Coast, Long Island.
Founded: 1644
Population: 2,770

Home of
The Most Famous Forgotten Poet in America

THE BRYANT LIBRARY

William Cullen Bryant
Famous Forgotten Poet
(1794 - 1878)

William Cullen Bryant became a literary sensation at the age of 23 for composing a poem that was proclaimed by critics to be so deep, so subtle, and so high-minded that it was the long-awaited proof that America could produce art equal to Europe.

Bryant's famous poem, *Thanatopsis*, comprises 81 lines about mankind's excruciating fear of death, along the lines of

The golden sun,
The planets, all the infinite host of
heaven,
Are shining on the sad abodes of death
[etc.]

Thanatopsis, 1817

The poem is morose, and preachy, and has a full set of Thee's, Thy's, Thine's, and Thou's... in other words, it's a poem that was perfectly in tune with the tastes of its time.

Being a poet who is *famous* and being a poet *who can pay his bills* are two different things. So William Cullen Bryant monetized his literary skills and became a newspaperman. As Editor-in-Chief and part owner of the *New York Evening Post*, Bryant became an immensely powerful media mogul and the most influential opinion-maker of his day. He also became very, very rich.

Seize the Day

America's most famous poet moved to Roslyn in
1843 and settled down on 200 acres (81 hectares) of
highlands overlooking the Long Island Sound.
He called his estate Cedarmere.

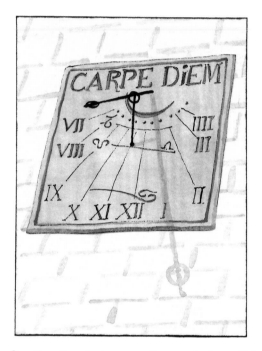

Reading the shadows on the vertical sundial
mounted on the southern façade of the Bryant
Public Library, you can see that it is a sunny
afternoon in early October. This is prime time to go
visit Cedarmere at its best.
So let us *Carpe Diem*.

William Cullen Bryant made the most of his popularity with the masses *and* with intellectuals by championing progressive democratic values such as the abolition of slavery and equal rights for women. He spearheaded the creation of Central Park and was instrumental in the founding of the National Academy of Design and the Metropolitan Museum of Art.

On February 7, 1860, Bryant gathered his inner circle of wealthy New York acquaintances at Cooper Union to introduce to them a little-known lawyer from Illinois named Abraham Lincoln. That audience then bankrolled Lincoln's winning run for the Presidency of the United States, which was the first major victory for the new, liberal party that William Cullen Bryant had co-founded: the Republicans.

Cedarmere
Home of William Cullen Bryant

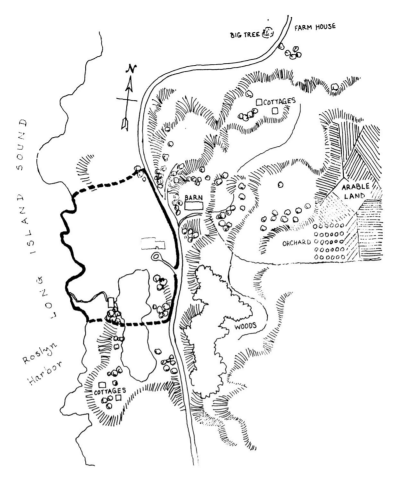

In 1975, William Cullen Bryant's great-granddaughter donated the last remaining seven acres (4 hectares) of the original 200-acre Cedarmere estate to the Nassau County Department of Parks, Recreation, and Museums.

In 2004 Cedarmere was included in the New York State Underground Railroad Heritage Trail.

The Friends of Cedarmere is a volunteer, nonprofit organization whose activities are essential to the ongoing restoration and preservation of the Cedarmere estate and gardens.

This is
William Cullen Bryant's
wooded *mere*.

This is how to curate
a small woods for
maximum
Autumn impact.

European Beech

Black Walnut

Chinese Scholar

Kentucky Coffee

Tulip

American White and
                Red Oaks

Turkish Oak
    (from Greece)

Honey Locust

Pignut Hickory

American Maples

Japanese Maples

Red Cedar

*The trees of
Cedarmere present
a curious combination
of natural wildness
and artificial planting.*

Anonymous, published in
The Art Journal For 1876

I roam the woods
Where mingled splendors glow,
Where the gay company
          of trees look down
On the green fields below.

Autumn Woods
William Cullen Bryant

Autumn on Long Island is
measured in hours, not days.
Even when the season is at its
brightest, we all know that
every gust of wind pushes us
closer toward the ragged days
of November and the long, cold
nights of Winter.
There is not a moment to lose
on a sunny afternoon in October
to find the perfect Fall leaf.

1

The criteria for a **Perfect Fall Leaf** is that it must tell its story in every color of the season.

Plus it has to have **personality**.

2

3

4

You'll know it when you see it.

5

And then you have to act fast -- these things never last long.

6

8

7

My 80-year-old neighbor likes to have company with her afternoon cocktail and so do I. She mixes up a batch of Rob Roys whenever we get together, and we settle in on her porch chairs and talk about all the other neighbors, living and dead.

One day my neighbor told me a story about an ancient bachelor who lived in the village, known as Old Mr. Treadwell. Old Mr. Treadwell was a friend of her father's and she remembered visiting Old Mr. Treadwell in his garden when she was a small girl. She said that the ancient gentleman used to entertain his guests by pointing to a small scraggly tree to announce, *That's the last of the Cedarmeres -- grown from the seed of the pear that Mr. Bryant himself gave me seventy years ago.*

William Cullen Bryant was exceedingly fond of pears.

Every August, when his prized pear trees were fruiting, William Cullen Bryant invited all the children of Roslyn to his estate for a cake-and-pears picnic. Mrs. Bryant's sponge cake was rumored to be only so-so, but the pears were a real treat.

When Old Mr. Treadwell was five years old he went up to Cedarmere for that cake-and-pears picnic. He too was exceedingly fond of pears, and the story goes that on that day, Mr. Bryant came upon young Old Mr. Treadwell crying in the orchard. The rule at Mr. Bryant's cake-and-pears picnic was that a child could gather up as many pears from the ground as he wanted, but the fruit in the trees had to be left untouched. However, the young Old Mr. Treadwell didn't want any of the wind-fallen pears on the ground -- he wanted the pear that was hanging in the tree above, just out of his reach.

It was Mr. Bryant's own special cultivar, the Cedarmere.

Mr. Bryant had a soft spot for children so he plucked the pear from the tree and gave it to the young Old Mr. Treadwell.

Mr. Bryant instructed the young Old Mr. Treadwell to take the pear home and put it in a cool, dark place until it was the color of a late Summer hay field. That's when it would be ripe enough to eat.

And that's the pear that gave the seed that made the tree that grew in the garden of Old Mr. Treadwell. But probably not.

From what little I know about pears, I spot a few holes in Old Mr. Treadwell's story. For one thing, you can't grow a Cedarmere Pear from the seeds of a Cedarmere Pear. It's just not possible to grow true-to-name fruit from seed. It's strange, but it's just the way fruit trees work. It would take cuttings, and seedlings, and graftings to grow a Cedarmere Pear tree and even then, the tree would have been long past its two score and ten year life span by the time Old Mr. Treadwell claimed that it was the last of the Cedarmere Pears.

Yet, here I am, re-telling this tall tale. I tell it because it's a story that thrills me to the core. It's my *living link* to William Cullen Bryant, from Old Mr. Treadwell's boast to that afternoon I sat on my neighbor's front porch, when Mr. Bryant had already been dead for more than a century and a half.

My neighbor and I hoisted our Rob Roys in a toast to my hero, America's Most Famous Forgotten Poet.

Otts, Jargonelle, Tyson,
Osband's Summer, Dearborn

After poetry,
William Cullen Bryant's *raison d'etre* was
pears.

In his orchard Mr. Bryant grew pears of the connoisseur
ilk (see above). He kept rows of pear-ripening chests in
his study and from mid-Summer to early Fall, the house
was filled with the distinct aroma of the process, a scent
of stale wine and rot that many of his visitors did not
find the least bit appealing.

Mr. Bryant's cultivar, the Cedarmere Pear, was small,
round, and greenish-yellow; its innards were juicy, white,
and fine-grained. The Cedarmere Pear last appeared in
the annals of the U. S. Department of Agriculture in 1908,
after which it presumably went extinct.

Mr. Bryant bequeathed Cedarmere to his daughter Julia,
who was not the pear-lover that her father was.
The orchard, left to die, became nothing but *pulvis et umbra,*
the *dust and shadow* that the ancient poet Horace said was
all that the good, the rich, and the famous, leave behind.

The great-granddaughter that Mr. Bryant never knew
was a very old lady when she turned over the house and
grounds to the stewardship of Nassau County.
By then, the orchard, long forgotten,
was known only by markings on old maps of the estate.

The quirky amnesia of history, the short half-life of
fame, the inevitable obscurity of one generation to
another...for whatever reason,
William Cullen Bryant is now as forgotten as
his beloved orchard.

The William Cullen Bryant Gardening Tip:
Seize the Day

No line of his poetry survives in the consciousness of his nation.

Frank Gado,
William Cullen Bryant: An American Voice

Edgar Allan Poe and Walt Whitman were both certain that Bryant's poetic genius would make him a *belles lettres* immortal.

Charles Dickens announced that the only man he wished to meet on his 1867 visit to New York City was William Cullen Bryant.

Abraham Lincoln, back in Illinois after that career-changing evening at Cooper Union hosted by Bryant, said, "It was worth the journey to the East merely to see such a man."

When Mr. Bryant died in 1878, every flag in New York City was lowered to half-mast.

The dedication speech for the colossal Bryant Memorial in Bryant Park in Manhattan, on October 24, 1911, was given by Henry Van Dyke, a renowned American intellectual who regularly lectured on Bryant's poetry at the Sorbonne.

That's how insanely famous the most famous forgotten poet in America used to be.

Anyone who knew him or knew *of* him back then would be astonished, and probably a bit disgusted, that such a man could be so little remembered today.

Even if his poetry has long ago gone out of fashion, it should be remembered that William Cullen Bryant was an heroic seizer of the day.

By any reckoning of his 82 years on Earth -- taking into account the number and quality of his achievements as a social and cultural activist, as a political idealist, and as a pomologist, it is clear that William Cullen Bryant could get a lot done in a day. Over a lifetime, that adds up. So while his name is no longer attached to the legacy of his good works, his humanitarianism still lives on, albeit anonymously, in the endurance of a nation that is of the people, by the people, and for the people.

To visit his Cedarmere home on a brilliant October afternoon is to experience the presence of what Mr. Bryant called the *still lapse of ages* -- the silence, the spaciousness, the *all-beholding* of the passing seasons. Thanatopsis: Every Autumn leaf is a reminder that the season of death lurks in every bright shining moment of life. Seize as many of those moments as you can, while you can.

Over a lifetime, they add up to a life well lived.

Edinburgh

Moments of Truth in a Winter Garden

So many inhabited solitudes...

...Scotland is the country above all others that I have seen, in which a man of imagination may carve out his own pleasures.

I feel more strongly the power of nature over me, and am better ... able to find enjoyment in what unfortunately to many persons is either dismal or insipid.

Dorothy Wordsworth, *Recollections of a Tour Made in Scotland*, 1803

Scotland is more than the land of introverts.
It is also the land *for* introverts.

I love being in my favorite foreign city when the days are half-lit and glazed
by a cold Winter rain. I am a connoisseur of rain (all us introverts are), and January
rain in Edinburgh is the rain of romance. It's for those of us who love the quiet of
libraries, the minor third of a sad song, and the aloneness of a 4 o'clock twilight.
If you happen to be a person who does not enjoy your own company,
a visit to Edinburgh in January will teach how it's done.

I must have walked past here seven or eight times
before I noticed it, that shimmer of green at No. 137.
At the end of this nondescript *close*, squeezed between an open-all-
year Christmas shop and a going-out-of-business travel agency, is
The Best Kept Secret in Edinburgh.

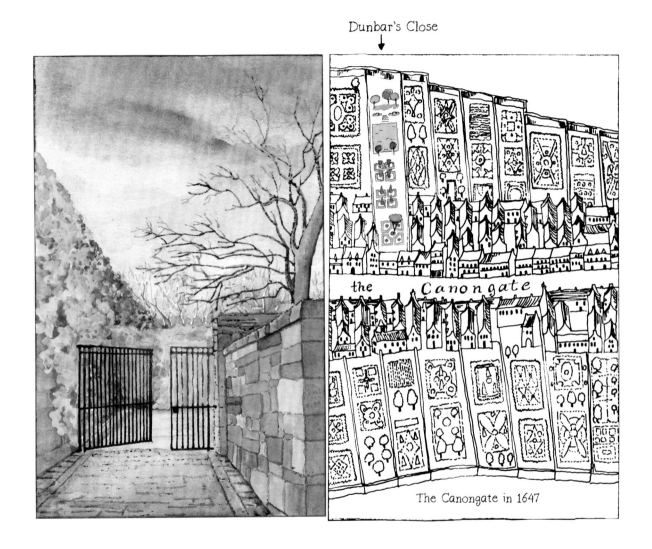

Dunbar's Close

the Canongate

The Canongate in 1647

Welcome to Dunbar's Close Garden
The only Baroque garden on the Canongate
" Laid Out in the Character of 17ᵗʰ Century Edinburgh "

125

Situate your garden in healthy soyl, defended from impetuous west winds, northern colds, and eastern blasts; the trees and shrubs at the wall well plyed and prun'd, the greens thereon cut in several figures, the walkes layed with gravel, and kept all clean and handsome.

The Scots Gard'ner
John Reid of Edinburgh, 1683

The Canongate was once the most elegant stretch of road in the Scottish kingdom. In its heyday, two Dukes, seven Barons, and sixteen Earls lived side by side to thirteen Baronets and seven Lords of Session.

However, the 18th and 19th centuries were not kind to the neighborhood.

As the gentry departed to more up-to-date quarters, the old mansions they left behind were turned into breweries, factories, tenements, and poorhouses.

Urban renewal, beginning in the 1950s, has halted the area's deterioration. The Canongate has been slowly returning to its former glory as a prestigious residential address in Edinburgh, despite the 2004 construction of the new Scottish Parliament on its lower end, which is surely one of the ugliest buildings in all of Europe.

Dunbar's Close Garden is the creation of The Mushroom Trust, a Scottish charity dedicated to the preservation of green spaces in urban areas.

The garden was designed by Seamus Filor, who later became a renowned lecturer of landscape architecture at the University of Edinburgh.

The Mushroom Trust donated the garden, "laid out in the character of 17th century Edinburgh", to the City of Edinburgh Council in 1978. This, or any garden "laid out in the character of 17th century Edinburgh" means one thing: High Baroque parterres.

A gardener in the 17th century had very little to work with. The colorful variety of flowers that we take for granted today did not exist back then, and there were only three ornamental evergreens native to Scotland -- Yew, Holly, and Scotch Pine. A fourth evergreen would fill out the planting list only if the gardener could get his hands on some imported Mediterranean Bay Laurel.

So the cleverest gardeners cultivated whatever plants they had at hand, and fashioned them into the amusing forms and patterns of the *parterre*.

The parterre combines the soothing meditative qualities of intricate geometry with the entertainment value of topiary.

And there you have it.

The WOW Factor.

Urban Gardening c. 1650 at its Best

By design you cannot rush your experience of this garden. The Baroque
formality has a way of sedating rambunctious visitors, and the narrow gravel
paths inhibit speedy passage from one garden room to the next.

For a garden of pleasure, rightly
made up and planted well,

will secure the ground within

from all that is hurtful

and will hide the ruggedness that
happeneth [outwith].

Box

Bay

Yew

Holly

Light Without Shadow

To see a tree in Winter is to see it for what it really is. A Winter tree is an object so intricate and so perplexing that if it hadn't already been decided that Winter trees were plain and boring, we would be spending hours pondering them, staring at them in astonishment.

Is the tree a completely random structure, or is there some logic to it? The solid trunk of a tree splits itself into branches, and the branches divide and divide again, seemingly by chance, and then all the branches arrive at the end of their dividing, as if at some pre-arranged destination, and in the end they hold in place the shape of something, up in the air, the outline of something, something that looks like the soul of the tree. Now *that's* a something worth considering.

And the evergreens! Instead of blending into the background, as they tend to do the rest of the year, the evergreens suddenly become conspicuous as the most alive things in the landscape. The truth of their warrior nature that they hide so well in warm weather is, in Winter, undeniable. There is no possibility of prevarication in the light of a Winter day.

Winter brings out the best in a Baroque garden. The honesty of the season exposes the true intentions of the garden's design. Winter reveals the arithmetic logic of straight lines and circles; the comforting symmetry that signals a psychological immunity to change; the pure, unalterable geometry of planes and solid figures that Socrates called *eternally and absolutely beautiful.*

The Scots Gard'ner
Winter Kalendar

Sharpen and mend tools.
Secure choice plants as yet from cold and wet.
Cover the roots of trees layed bair.
Shelter tender evergreen seedlings.

Prune firrs, plant haw-thorn hedges, and all
trees and shrubs that lose the leaf.
Also prune the more hardie and old-planted.

Feed weak bees.

Gather seeds of holly, yew, &c, for if you
desire trees worth your while, raise them
from the seed.
Gather oziers and hassell rods and make
baskets in stormy weather.

GARDEN DISHES AND DRINKS IN SEASON
Blanched sellery, pickled asparagus, colworts,
beet-rave, fennel roots in broth.
Cyder, wine of apples, pears, sherries, honey &c.

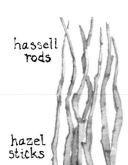

hassell
rods

hazel
sticks

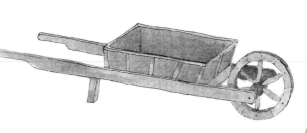

oziers

willow
twigs

There ought to be a word for the Winter form of a tree

It is highly unusual to find a tulip tree in a small parterre as it is better situated for a much grander landscape.

Tulip trees were a sensation as soon as they started to appear in British gardens, when they were first brought over from the American colonies in the 1630s. Tulip trees were highly prized for their shapely leaves, golden Autumn color, and stately form. Mature trees average 80 to 100 feet (24-30 meters) in height with a 40 foot (12 meter) crown. Tulip trees are still one of the most popular shade trees in the U.K.

However, a Tulip tree in 17th century Scotland would have been an extremely rare sight. The Scottish economy was severely depressed. One English pound was worth four Scottish ones, which would have made foreign trade outrageously expensive … but since when has cost ever deterred an obsessive collector from getting what he wants? The c. 1630 cost of a Tulip sapling was equal to six months of a gardener's wages.

It's four o'clock
in the afternoon.
The light is almost gone.
Closing time
at Dunbar's Close.

About the sheltered garden ground
The trees stand strangely still.
The vale never seemed so deep before,
Nor yet so high the hill.

An awe-full sense of quietness,
A fullness of repose,
Breathes from the dewy garden lawns,
The silent garden rows.

Robert Louis Stevenson,
Edinburgh native son

Edinburgh Gardening Tip:
Inhabit Your Solitude

This shade of green should not exist so far from the tropics, and certainly not in the dead of Winter. Scottish fescue: it loves a cold soaking rain.

It's been a *dreich* day, I am thoroughly *drookit*. It rains 250 days a year in Scotland, so the Scots -- no surprise here -- have quite a lot of words to describe *rain* and *getting rained on.*

At this far northern latitude the sun sets very, very slowly. The January twilight will be with us for about three-quarters of an hour, plenty of time to get acquainted with the old souls that inhabit the misty light. In Scotland this time of day is called *the gloaming.*

I am profoundly pleased to have the last garden room all to myself. The chill is bracing, the stone walls stand watch. The roar of the world is far, far way. Any person of imagination would gladly inhabit this aloneness. I mean, really; is silence and solitude so hard to bear?

As a matter of fact, most people find the silence and solitude of one's own company to be excruciating. Six minutes, max, (it's a scientific fact) is the amount of quiet me-time that most people can tolerate before they have to find something to do, watch, text, or update. These fidgety people are the people I want to bring to Dunbar's Close in January.

The garden's austere design and the simplicity of the season make for about as unadorned a garden experience as possible. From parterre to parterre, there's nothing to distract your attention from the fact that it's just you, the garden, and the path. Inhabiting the moment of you, the garden, and the path, as completely as possible, as is feasible only in a garden such as Dunbar's Close in January, is a sure way to feel secure from within, secure and safe from all that is hurtful and rugged that happens outwith.

London

Physic Gardening for a Remembrance of Things Past

The More Things Change
The Less They Stay the Same

Travel was cheap and the Sex Pistols were dangerous when I visited London for the first time, back when a room in a shabby Georgian town house-turned-B&B in Chelsea cost me a mere £5 a night. My Bed & Breakfast on Oakley Street was just around the corner from London's hippest avenue, Kings Road, back when it was the epicenter of punk -- the *real* punk, the shocking, filthy, political, poor people's punk. I was a 20-year old from the suburbs of Philadelphia and I walked up and down King's Road in a state of wonder. The faces pierced with safety pins and the tattered clothes held together with chains were things I'd only seen in photographs. A Monty Python walked right past me, wearing a full length fur coat and a top hat with feathers. Maybe it was a beret. It was a long time ago. And it was all *so cool.*

But that is so last century. Since then, punk has become merely a fashion statement, and Chelsea is now the epicenter of chic. Princess Diana shopped for silk waistcoats and gold jewelry here, and my old £5-a-night bedroom is now a renovated minimalist studio apartment (what they call a *bedsit* in England) available on a £198,000 leasehold. The times have certainly changed.

I changed too, into a thirty-something who traveled to London only now and then for long weekend holidays. As a houseguest, my favorite place to be was with an American ex-pat who lived in one of those old Georgian townhouses, spiffed-up to meet the area's high standards.

My host's third-floor balcony had an impressive marble balustrade and a view of the neighborhood that fit, *to a T,* the idea of London that I'd held in my heart since childhood. The balcony overlooked a block of gracious homes and gardens that were straight out of the tales of Peter Pan, Mary Poppins, and Paddington Bear. There was also a bit of Sherlock Holmes and Bertie Wooster in there. And a touch of Lord Peter Wimsy. I've read a lot of English classics.

It's important to know that in all of England, one's backyard is called *the garden.* Even if it's only a small patch of turf behind a tenement, it's still *the garden.* The gardens on view from that third-floor balcony were a decidedly whimsical sight, each walled in from one another like so many miniature fiefdoms.

There are a good number of such walls bricking up the gardens of Chelsea. But there was only one wall that made me crazy with curiosity.

The word is *circummured*.

Swan Walk, Chelsea; a quiet lane near the
Thames River, bordered by a 350-year-old wall.
It took me a decade to figure out how to get myself
into the garden concealed behind that wall.
Yes, I was aware that all it took was buying an
entrance ticket, but that was not as easy as it sounds.

The garden gate, opened at last.

Welcome to the

Chelsea Physic Garden.

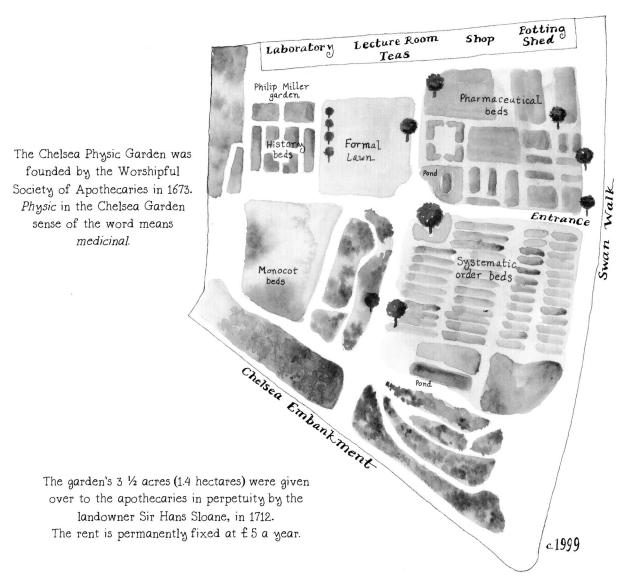

The Chelsea Physic Garden was founded by the Worshipful Society of Apothecaries in 1673. *Physic* in the Chelsea Garden sense of the word means *medicinal.*

The garden's 3 ½ acres (1.4 hectares) were given over to the apothecaries in perpetuity by the landowner Sir Hans Sloane, in 1712. The rent is permanently fixed at £ 5 a year.

The Chelsea Physic Garden went public only in 1983, when it became a registered charity and *had* to open its doors to the masses. Not that that made it any easier to get into. As I remember, the visiting hours back then were a few hours on Monday morning, different hours on Wednesday, and an hour or two on Thursday. It was not easy to synchronize this random availability with my infrequent trips to London. In 1999 I bettered the garden's vexing anti-public openings and voilá: the garden was mine!

The pecking order
of the 17th century
health care system went like this:

Physicians Highly educated in superstitions both ancient and "modern"; concerned only with diagnosis and prescription. Charged ten shillings for services.

Surgeons Despised by the physician for their lowly craft; chief sources of income were bloodlettings and amputations.

Barbers Fees higher than surgeons, but status much lower. Extracted teeth and performed other minor maxillofacial procedures.

Apothecaries Usually dirt poor, peddled medical ingredients along with cosmetics and sweets. Broke away from the Grocer's Company* in 1617 to form the Worshipful Society of Apothecaries. In 1673 the Society founded a private physic garden for the formal training of apprentice apothecaries in the identification and uses of healing herbs and plants. This enabled apothecaries to rise to a semi-professional status that put them on a par with surgeons.

REGISTERED CHARITY No. 286513

ADMIT ONE

Chelsea Physic Garden
FOUNDED 1673

LIMITED COMPANY
REGISTERED IN ENGLAND
No. 1690871

N⁰ 56704

* Important note: Why bother writing a book if you can't right a neologistic wrong in a footnote?
  The word **grocer** is a middle-English word meaning *one who sells by the gross.* The word **grocery** was first used in the sense of *a grocer's shop* in the mid-18th century. Both words derive from the Latin root *grossus.* It is therefore incorrect to pronounce either word with a *sh* sound. So please stop doing it.
  Thank you.

Important Things to Know About the Chelsea Physic Garden

The Chelsea Physic Garden has been in constant cultivation since 1673. From its auspicious inauguration as a teaching garden, it eventually became renowned as the richest and most exotic collection of healing and ornamental plants in all of Europe. Its phenomenal biological diversity was made possible by its walls.

The walls shelter against harsh weather but more importantly, they also trap heat, giving the Physic Garden a fecund micro-climate that is able to support tropical *and* alpine plant growth in the heart of London.

As early as 1685 the garden had a thriving Cinchona tree from the Andean tropics, used for the production of anti-malarial quinine, at that time a very rare and expensive medicine. In later years the gardeners grew other exotic species from South America, such as the *Brugmansia arborea* from Chile, which is now extinct in the wild.

The garden was the first to successfully cultivate a pineapple in England, and it still boasts the northern-most fruiting grapefruit tree. The earliest botanical specimens from the American colonies were successfully propagated here, and it was the first foreign home of the Madagascar periwinkle -- now the chief ingredient for certain anti-leukemia alkaloids.

Believe me, I was as bored writing this (above) as you were reading it, and I could go on and on about the discoveries and science, and the eccentric and brilliant curators and gardeners who in the course of its 350-year history shaped the destiny of the Chelsea Physic Garden from its humble beginnings as a trade school for quacks to one of the most significant research and development gardens in the Western world. But I won't.

I think that with this brief overview (above), I have done my duty as your garden guide and now I can get on with what really matters to me about my Chelsea Physic Garden experience. Its delicious decrepitude.

I had no idea of what to expect from a walled-in physic garden in Chelsea.
But this grand scene of stately dilapidation did not disappoint.

Don't take this the wrong way,
but the Chelsea Physic Garden was a wreck.

The Chelsea Physic Garden looked to be exactly the kind of genteel but decrepit garden that an English literature-loving gal like me would expect to find behind a mysterious but terribly grand ancient garden hiding in the heart of London.

The herb and culinary beds scented the air like gently rotting wild thickets of potpourri, which is also what they looked like; gently rotting wild thickets of tall grass and falling-apart barky things with some shriveled flowers thrown into the mix.

The Woodland Garden contained a small but valiant stand of English trees, drooping under the weight of a gloomy overgrowth of a viney sort that looked and, when you stood under it, felt medieval.

The pathways in the Garden of Medicine had been worn down into very narrow strips of gravel between rows of raucous vegetation, mostly unmarked except for signs that warned POISON. *How very Agatha Christie,* I remember thinking.

Also, the place was practically empty and I roamed the grounds like a ghost.

I loved it.

Decrepitude has character, dilapidation has soul. There is great dignity in a regal decay.

And then I saw a sign for the Chelsea Physic Garden Tea Room.

It was the only thing that could have made me love this place even more. Tea.

And so it was that, on a September afternoon, surrounded by the scent of sweet herbs and blight, I sat myself down on a folding chair in the English sunshine and took a forkful of glazed orange cake (homemade by the volunteers who staffed the Physic Garden Tea Room) and a sip of freshly-brewed Assam tea (ditto) and I knew this was the perfection I'd been searching for. This was it. My Happy Place.

And then I went on with my life, blithely assuming that there would always be cake and tea and decrepitude in my Happy Place.

Dear Readers, *that's* the Chelsea Physic Garden I wanted to write about.

But I have the unhappy task, Dear Readers, of telling you that *that* Chelsea Physic Garden no longer exists.

150

Things have changed a lot at the Chelsea Physic Garden.

A new team of brilliant curators and head gardeners has redesigned the old place to make it dazzlingly relevant for the 21st century.

The dank bits that once looked like horticultural scrapheaps have been cleared out for exhibits that show the latest research in taxonomy, phylogeny, and biochemistry. Newly re-planted beds offer ethno-horticultural interpretations of medicinal, edible, and commercial plants that still come to the Physic from around the world.

The Woodland Garden has been tidied up and linked to three new areas of cultivated wilderness that, all together, create an educational and adorable half-acre micro-forest.

There's a Wollemi Pine snuggled up against a warm brick wall.

And finally, they have done something with the dilapidated rock garden.

As well as being the oldest planted rock garden in England, the Chelsea Physic rockery was once universally acknowledged as also being the ugliest rock garden in Europe.

When I last saw it many years ago, I found it endearing that the rock garden was little more than a soggy mound of earth set with an array of unattractive rubble and a haphazard assortment of scraggly plants. There was a stagnant puddle of scum positioned atop the mound, encased by a weather-beaten black plastic tarp.

Alas. The mangy old rock garden has been completely excavated and re-turfed, and the old rock bits (which are historic in their own right) have been sorted and thoughtfully re-set in naturalistic groupings. The rancid puddle is now a beautifully situated oval pool of blue water, and the plantings, all accurate to the vision of the original rock garden, are exuberant with form and texture. There is even moss. The rockery is now one of the garden's main attractions.

Under a new policy of inclusiveness, the Chelsea Physic Garden is open 40 hours a week, even in Winter, and even on Sundays. It's also available for hire, on weekday evenings and all day every Saturday, for very posh private events and lavish weddings.

Visitors now flock to the place like never before.

The Chelsea Physic Garden has, in a word, been *discovered* as one of the top gardens in Britain.

London Gardening Tip:
Accept Change

What I would most like to revisit in the Chelsea Physic Garden is the old Tea Room. It used to be housed in a small box-shaped room that had pale pink walls and a drab gray carpet. There were two rows of tables, each covered with oilcloth, lined up like a school cafeteria.

A table at the head of the room was set with dozens of paired cups and saucers, and another table displayed cakes baked that morning in the home kitchens of the kindly Tea Room Lady volunteers. Each cake was sliced into 16ths. The lighting was fluorescent.

I believe that a cup of tea with a portion of cake cost £1, and all proceeds supported the English Gardening School, whose classroom door was located just behind the cake table.

That's the Tea Room that I wanted to be there forever, at the Chelsea Physic Garden.

But of course it's long gone. Now there's a cream-walled/blond wood/natural light flooded restaurant called the Tangerine Dream. The menu is a fusion of Italian, European, and classic British cuisine, and the food has been called *heaven on earth* by the *Daily Mail*.

Sunday brunch is usually crowded with the garden's posh neighbors, and I hear that the orange polenta cake is to *die* for. There is a delightful outdoor terrace for those who wish to dine *al fresco*. A typical lunch for two, with wine, goes for £50 -- quite the bargain in Chelsea these days.

In addition to tea, the Tangerine Dream also serves champagne, beer, and wine.

There comes an age, usually not long after your 30th birthday, when you begin to notice that the pace of social change is leaving you behind. Singers you've never heard of score Number One hit songs that you've never heard of. Fashion trends become so ridiculous that you wonder who on Earth would wear them. Your teen idol has grandchildren.

That's when nostalgia becomes your coping mechanism for getting through life. That's when you become a nuisance to others and a bore to yourself every time you say, *This used to be...I remember when... In my day....*

So what if the Chelsea Physic Garden has re-defined itself by breaking with tradition and revising all the old tried-and-true ways. Did I mention that you can now get a glass of champagne to go with your visit? And of course the past decade has transformed these four golden acres in Chelsea. That only makes these four acres no different from any other four acres in the world. Things change. Deal with it.

I can live with change. Especially when it is served with champagne.

Rio de Janeiro

The Once in a Lifetime Midnight Garden

I had to pack like a grown up:
dresses, good shoes, nice jewelry.
It was June, so I also stuffed a
Winter coat into my suitcase.

I didn't know a soul in Rio de Janeiro, but I knew that I'd be
meeting *plenty* of interesting people once I got there.
I was travelling as the assistant to a debonair English decorative
arts expert. He would be my guide to Brazil, and he'd also be
doing most of the talking -- he had a posh English accent and,
even in a Portuguese-speaking country, people *love* that.
By the way, 69°F (21°C) is the average June temperature in Rio.
Only a doofus would have packed a Winter coat.
Pleeeeeeeze, I begged of myself, *don't do anything stupid in front
of your boss in the next eight days*.
Gardening was not on the agenda.

156

Most of Rio's seven million inhabitants live
in the North Zone, but it's the *Zona Sul* that
is famous around the world for its fabulous
Atlantic Ocean beach communities.

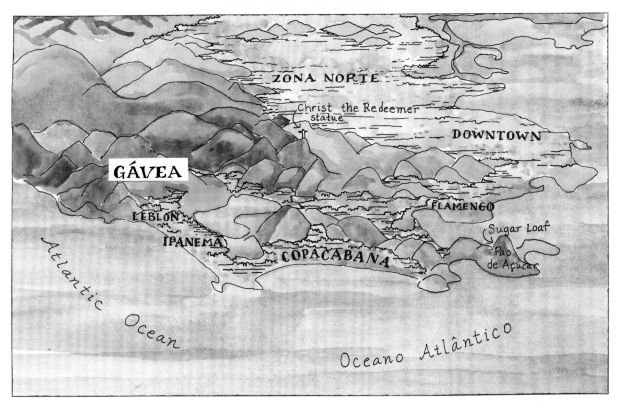

What I *now* know about Rio is that the seacoast
communities of Leblon and Ipanema are where
you go to meet billionaire collectors
of de Lamerie silver and Fabergé what-nots.

Gávea is an affluent, hilly district on the edge
of a jungle where the capuchin monkey and
tufted-eared marmoset roam.
Gávea is where you go if you are in search of
Brazilian intellectuals with renounced Braganza
titles and unforgettable midnight gardens.

By night there were *Zona Sul* parties that lasted into the wee hours. By day there were business meetings to appraise private hoards of Georgian epergnes and Romanov *objets*.

All I know of Sugarloaf Mountain, Copacabana, and Flamengo is what I saw of them from penthouse apartments. I highly recommend the billionaire's view of Rio.

That said, I met only one *rich* person while I was in Rio. In England, my English boss told me, "rich" means something that "wealthy" does not. Self-made billionaires are *wealthy*, but only a Duke can be *rich*. That's just how the English language works in its native land.

The rich gentleman I met in Rio was a celebrated intellectual with an historic last name. I had no idea that he was also quite the gardener until I attended a dinner party that he gave in his home, in Gávea. After all the other guests had cleared out, his wife and her favorite English decorative arts expert were having a *tête-à-tête* about the latest news concerning the Three D's of international high society -- Death, Debt, and Divorce -- so our host invited me to step outside for a walk in his garden. With us came the family dog, a goofy, sweet-natured mixed-breed lummox whom my host had named after himself.

Because of my host (author of books against
capitalism and for critical pedagogy) and the
house he lived in (ultra-modernist concrete)
I prepared myself for a rather formal garden
experience in this backyard in Gávea.
But that's not even close to what I got.
This garden was like nothing I'd ever seen.

The Poinsettia Tree
Where I come from, poinsettias are small,
disposable houseplants. A towering poinsettia *tree*,
its branches sifting a June moonlight as cool as
January, was a set of circumstances that I had
never envisioned.
This now strikes me as a pitiful lack of
imagination on my part.

What Made Me Think of Rousseau

Henri Rousseau spent his entire life in France.
But between visits to the *Jardin des Plantes* and the
Paris zoo, Rousseau deduced that he lived in a
world that was too wonderful for words.
So he became a painter of jungles,
lush, dreamlike, voluptuous.
There was a bit of that going on all around me.

I couldn't help but be awed.

I had never been in a jungle before.

No, my host said, *this is not the jungle*. However (he said) the territorial instincts of the rainforest jungle that surrounded us were quite powerful. He welcomed the wildness that lived and breathed in every corner of his backyard garden (he said) as the life force of the once-powerful Atlantic Forest, impatient to re-claim its dominion.

The Atlantic Forest was once a massive ecosystem that covered 330 million acres (133 million hectares) of eastern Brazil, from Recife to the Argentine border.

Mere slivers of the Forest remain intact today (estimated at 7% of the original), the result of five centuries of human settlement and plunder. The worst of it was the pillage of an endemic tree known as the Pau-Brasil. The Pau-Brasil became the Atlantic Forest's most lucrative export because its sap produced the most brilliant red dye available in the centuries before the industrial revolution.

These days, its dark dense wood is in high demand for making top quality bows for stringed instruments. Now, as a result of incessant logging, the Pau-Brasil one of the most endangered trees in the world.

The Pau-Brasil happens to be the national tree of Brazil. It is the very reason why we even have a "Brazil" in the first place. Because of its massive trade in the Pau-Brasil tree, early mapmakers took to calling the entire country simply **Brasil**.

In 1861 Emperor Dom Pedro II called a halt to the deforestation of the land surrounding Rio de Janeiro. On 8,000 acres (3,200 hectares) in Gávea, he ordered the planting of 100,000 seedling trees. In straight lines.

The old jungle, which had been lying in wait for 350 years, lost no time devouring the Emperor's grid. The area is now a wilderness in the exact image of the Atlantic Forest, a place where 54% of its trees, 64% of its palms, 74% of its bromeliads, and 30% of its orchids are found nowhere else in the world.

Mata
Atlântica

Zygopetalum
mackayi Hooker

Laelia
purpurata

Brazil wood
pau brasil

Atlantic
Forest

Worsleya procera

It's the way you feel when you listen to the singing of night birds, look up to see the blue glow of the Southern Cross, and inhale the cool celery scent of moon ... and you know that no night will ever be like this again.
Brazilians call this feeling **saudade**.

In Brazil, *saudade* is the spice of life

The Summer vacations of childhood, the *fejoada* of a dearly departed grandmother, a first kiss -- what they all have in common is a Brazilian remembering them with affection and sighing *Que saudade*.

This is how Brazilians express their humanity, in one word: *Saudade*.

For every Brazilian I have known, it's a point of pride that *saudade* (sah-oo-dah-zghe), defies translation. But I'm going to give it a try.

Saudade is: The desire for something that no longer exists, and probably cannot ever exist again.

Longing with the knowledge that there is no end to the longing.

A sentimental melancholy combined with a deep sense of loss.

The presence of absence.

The concept of *saudade* is such a key component in Brazilian culture that, for a foreigner to fully understand the soul of Brazil, it's important for them to fully understand *saudade*.

It's also said that the English translation of the bossa nova classic *The Girl From Ipanema* utterly misses the mark because it lacks the *saudade* of the original lyric composed by Carioca poet, the great Vinicius de Moraes.

So it seems that, on most days, Brazilians live to be sad.

And yet...

According to the World Happiness Report published by the United Nations in 2013, Brazilians are, compared to the 149 other countries in the poll, in the top tier of happiness. They are, in fact, 3.5 times happier than the Portuguese who, after all, invented *saudade* in the first place.

Three and a half times happier is the same difference between the United States and Uzbekistan. It's the difference between the U.K. and Libya. Something *really* sad must be going on in Portugal.

I know there lurks a lesson, in there, about the nature of happiness, how it is enriched by saudade; how pleasure is enhanced by a morsel of misery, or how joy cannot exist without its shadow of sorrow.

But I am more interested in finding out what *saudade* has to do with gardening in Rio.

Rio de Janeiro Gardening Tip:
Love the world.
Praise it with a garden.

I kept telling everyone, in the weeks following my trip to Brazil, *I stood under a poinsettia tree!*

And no one ever said **Wow**. Obviously, I wasn't telling it right.

So that's why I wrote this book.

You see, when you come back from Brazil and people ask you, *How was it?*, they really don't want to hear about plants. They want to hear how you stayed up all night doing the samba in the street, and the number of times you fell in love with a hunky Carioca, but not about a *Euphorbia pulcherrima* on the edge of the Atlantic Forest.

Unless you put it in context.

So I wrote this whole book just to put that garden experience in context, that very personal, one-to-one moment I had with Planet Earth that made me go *Wow!*

It's an experience that I imagine most gardeners are familiar with, but it took me standing under a poinsettia tree in a backyard jungle in Gávea that gave me my first experience of awe in the presence of an extraordinary plant. And since then I know that there isn't a grass, flower, weed, shrub, or tree that grows on this heavenly body that isn't extraordinary.

I can never go back to that midnight in the garden on the edge of the Atlantic Forest...*que saudade.*

But, happily, every great garden experience comes encoded with some little bit of that *Wow!* of a once-in-a-lifetime moon-lit Poinsettia Tree.

Ever since we first recognized ourselves as beings burdened with the mission of taking charge of this harsh, perplexing, seemingly pointless, and beautiful speck of dirt in the universe, our kind has been making gardens. No matter how grand or minuscule, every garden has a meaning all its own; but every garden, everywhere, has a common reason for being, in that it was made in homage to this wondrous Earth that has given life to every Eden we've ever imagined.

166

Acknowledgments

Paris -- Carol Gillott, for the spiffy new paint box.

Key West -- Jean Harrison, Arnold Hermelin, and all the crusaders of Save Our Pines, for never giving up.

Marrakech -- Sarah Quinn Ezzarghani, Moroccan by fate, for steering me away from the beaten track.

New Orleans -- Karen Kersting, Bad Dog, Little B, and Sloo, for gardening their patch of New Orleans back from disaster.

John P. Humes Japanese Stroll Garden -- The Garden Conservancy, for saving America's special spaces.

Cedarmere -- The Friends of Cedarmere, for keeping the Bryant legacy alive.

Edinburgh -- Rebecca Govier, Manager of Dunbar's Close, for ensuring its future; Jean Bareham, for setting me straight about secret garden botany; John Gilchrist, photographer extraordinaire, for his eye; and www.Edinburgh Spotlight.com, for their kind permission to use their image of the Close in snow.

London -- Mark Hesher, for his hospitality and his balcony view; Elizabeth Wix, for her portrait of the Chelsea Physic Garden, and for the tea and sympathy. (Hi Buster!)

Rio de Janeiro -- Christie's Auction House in New York, for sending me to the city where Poinsettias grow on trees.

Janet Lea -- for her coyote spirit: indomitable, insightful, and wise -- she always knows when the time is right for champagne.

Gitana Garofolo -- for the treasures she shares.

My deepest gratitude goes to **Betsy Lerner**, whose expert guidance made this book ten times better. When she tells you to cut out paragraphs of blabber *there*, and to add more exposition *here*, you better listen, is all I'm saying.